DOUBLE-SPEAK
IN
AMERICA

OTHER BOOKS BY *MARIO PEI*

All about Language
The America We Lost
The American Road to Peace
The Book of Place Names (with E. Lambert)
The Families of Words
First-Year French (with E. Méras)
Getting Along in French (with J. Fisher)
Getting Along in German (with R. Politzer)
Getting Along in Italian
Getting Along in Portuguese (with A. Prista)
Getting Along in Russian (with F. Nikanov)
Getting Along in Spanish (with E. Vaquero)
Glossary of Linguistic Terminology
How to Learn Languages and What Languages to Learn
Invitation to Linguistics
The Italian Language
Language for Everybody
The Language of the Eighth-Century Texts in Northern France
Language Today (with others)
The Many Hues of English
One Language for the World
Our Names (with E. Lambert)
Our National Heritage
The Story of Language
The Story of the English Language
Swords of Anjou
Tales of the Natural and Supernatural
Talking Your Way around the World
Voices of Man
What's in a Word?
Words in Sheep's Clothing
The World's Chief Languages

DOUBLE-SPEAK IN AMERICA

by Mario Pei

HAWTHORN BOOKS, INC.

PUBLISHERS / New York

Contents

DOUBLE-SPEAK
IN
AMERICA

1

Further Explorations in Weasel Words

It is now three years since I sounded my tocsin concerning *Words in Sheep's Clothing*. Similar and more elaborate alarms had been sounded before. One need only refer to the works of Wesley C. Salmon, Irving Lee, Wendell Johnson, I. A. Richards, Stuart Chase, S. I. Hayakawa, and, of course, Alfred Korzybski, who is regarded by many as the high priest of General Semantics.

My own modest contribution stressed what I chose to call Weasel Words, used and misused not through habit, inadvertence, or accident, but coined or distorted, and then put into circulation by deliberate design, for purposes of deception. Of these, a new and bountiful crop has sprung up.

This is not to say that I scorn what is accidental in word usage and word change, the fortuitous understatement or circumlocution, like the one attributed to the shy Irishman from County Kerry who, having kept company with a girl for thirty years, finally decided to pop the question. He couldn't bring himself to say, "Will you marry me?" So he worded it in a curious way that was a reflection of both individual mentality and national custom: "How would you like to be buried with my people?"

The words and phrases I particularly have in mind are differently defined and described by different writers. Thomas H. Barton, writing in *Think,* calls them "buzz words," because they make a pleasant buzzing sound in your ears but convey little meaning, yet have a conscious or unconscious purpose. His simpler examples run from "serendipity" to "programming," from "commitment" to "ghetto," from "charisma" to "hard-core." Despite his tolerant attitude, he admits that they can sometimes be harmful. Another writer speaks of "purr-r-r and grr-r-r words," those that soothe and put to sleep, and those that antagonize; but again, they may be largely accidental, as when Jean Stapleton of *All in the Family* recalls that in her early and innocent girlhood, having been sent out by her mother to buy a chicken, she asked the Italian Catholic butcher to "cut off the pope's nose." Bruce Price, in *Book World,* reports a proliferation of modifier nouns ("curriculum unit" for "course," "student population" for "students," "highway systems" for "highways") and attributes it to the fact that some people are not comfortable with whatever it is they are saying and feel the need to dress it up. But dress it up for whom? Themselves, or for their hearers or readers?

Complaints about the degeneration in the meaning and use of words often come from the clergy. The Rev. Eugene C. Blake, of the World Council of Churches, deplores the fact that the great Christian words are becoming threadbare: "charity" has degenerated into patronage of the poor by the rich; "love" is what goes on between movie stars;

"service" resolves itself into menial duties; "redemption" is applied to trading stamps; "gospel" is slang for truth. Bishop Fulton Sheen, still more outspoken, speaks of the new meaning of "conversion" as tearing down vertical relations to God for the sake of horizontal relations to neighbor; of "prayer" as action; of "piety" as fervor for social revolution; of "reconciliation" as linking hands for a common assault against society as presently constituted. "The poor," in his view, are those on whose behalf violence is exerted; but they must be "interesting" poor, such as the blacks in the United States or South Africa, the Viet Cong, or the Palestinian Arabs, not the "uninteresting" poor, such as the Tibetans, the Kurds, the Biafrans, or the East Pakistanis. "High-voltage words" offered in a list by the *Christopher News Notes* include "radical," "establishment," and authority"; "barrier words" are "conservative," "liberal," "prejudice"; "bridge-building words" are "balance," "dialogue," "respect." Users are cautioned to be accurate, fair, concise, careful, honest, and to be the masters, not slaves, of the words they use.

As against some largely accidental shifts in meaning, there are the intentional slants, distortions, and outright coinages inspired by a purpose of profit, propaganda, or, at the very least, personal or institutional prestige. The world of commercial advertising is naturally one of the heaviest contributors to this class of creations, but by its very nature it must also be the frankest. As one jokester has put it, "In this country streets aren't safe, parks aren't safe, subways aren't safe, but under our arms we have 'complete protection.' " "Brand name" always comes to the rescue; and you always recognize the hero by its familiar label.

In the field of politics, too, you generally know where you stand and who is coining your slogans for you. Public relations, which in essence is the art of using the right word (or perhaps we should say the most effective word, be it right or wrong), has permeated more fields than we care to contemplate, and in not all of them is the penetration obvious. Yet it is there: in the arts, in education and scholarship, in science, in economics, in labor relations, in finance. It is there in the grim business of warfare and defense, where it often takes the form of understatement, since the merchandise is death. Movements of all kinds (whether officially organized, like political parties; half-organized, like civil rights movements, antidefamation leagues, women's liberation groups; utterly disorganized, like the Youth Culture) reek of the language of public relations, a language designed to enhance a given cause in the eyes of the would-be indifferent, and force him to become "involved" and bestir himself on behalf of that cause.

In all of these fields, weasel word production has been brisk in the last three years, far beyond our expectations. It is therefore worthwhile to focus upon the latest batch so that you, as a potential hearer and reader, may be put on your guard. Whether you care to heed the warning is, of course, your own business.

2

The Wonder World of Advertising

High on Madison Avenue's legitimate agenda is the matter of brand names, with their concomitant patents. George Lazarus, in *Saturday Review*, reminds us that the U.S. Patent Office in Washington has well over 400,000 brand names registered, with the total swelling by over 20,000 each year.

Finding the "right name" for a product (that is, a name that will sell the product) constitutes the search for the name of the game, and according to a Gillette executive, it is "one king-sized headache." Yet products, like people, have to have names. Can those names be protected from others who covet them? Yes and no. Consider these former brand names that have now fallen into the common domain: scotch tape, shredded wheat, frigidaire, cellophane, nylon, aspirin, linoleum, thermos. Just as "mimeograph," once a brand name, is now used for all sorts of duplicating processes, so there is a strong likelihood that "Xerox" will go the same way. The competitor doesn't have to do a thing about it. All the name has to do is to catch the public fancy, and it becomes generalized. I was once approached by a Gillette representative who wanted to know if there was any way of inducing language academies, in the countries that boast such institutions, to proclaim that "gillette" (or *gilete*) should not be used as a generic name for safety razors, but be reserved for their own brand. The reply was that even if a language academy could be persuaded to make such a pronouncement, nobody would pay it the slightest attention.

 Often name coiners are unconcerned with the problem of exclusivity. *Women's Wear Daily* is credited with the creation of the term "hot pants" and its broadcasting into the entire clothing industry. Actually, "hot pants" is merely a new name for an existing object, which at an earlier date used to be known as "short shorts." It is my suspicion (unverified) that "hot pants" was coined as a crossing between "hot mamma" and "fancy (or smarty) pants," both with their roots in the past.

The labor, time, and ingenuity that go into the coining of suitable (i.e., selling) brand names are unbelievable. Computers as well as foreign language experts are put to work to make sure that the name under consideration will not convey unpleasant, ridiculous, or obscene connotations in the language of any of the countries where the product is to be marketed. "Con" Edison always sends French visitors into stitches. And an American tourist recently came back from France laughing about an orange drink produced there called "Pshit." The "P," of course, is silent. Long hours are spent in determining whether a new feminine deodorant spray should be labeled FDS or FD1 (why?). It has been statistically determined that the favorite component word for brand names is "magic" ("Magic Moment," "Hidden Magic," "Deep Magic," "Soft Magic," "Blue Magic," "Magic Flash"), with "king" as the runner-up ("King Vitaman"). The favorite suffix seems to be "plus" ("Platinum Plus Blades," "Orange Plus," "Instant Breakfast Plus," "Flavor Plus Dog Food"). Sometimes one wonders what dictated the choice. "Born Free" for a shampoo is not bad; it may even exert some charm on the Liberated Woman; but what induced the makers of a snack food to call it "Screaming Yellow Zonkers"? Kid appeal, perhaps? At times there is a clear intention to go along with a popular movement. Three new detergents, "Concern," "Savus," and "Ecolo-G," all promote a strong conservation image.

Stress on violence of a military nature is indicated by popular names of electronic pinball gizmos: "Airstrike," "Periscope," "Combat," "Missile," "Attack," "Tank Assault." Glamorous movie personalities are pressed into service by the advertising media. Japan, which is having a blue jeans fad, labels its product "Big John" and has a reproduction of John Wayne on the pants leg.

Government agencies are not above coining brand names, though competition is generally absent from the scene. "Amtrak" for the national passenger railroad network, for instance, was coined anonymously, winning out over such other suggested names as "Amspan" and "Easy Rider." Some say it is perilously close to the acronym "Amtrac," used for the amphibious-tracked vehicle used by the Marine Corps. But a survey showed that few people made the connection. My own fear was that there might be confusion with Hamtramck, a name of mysterious origin used for a section of Detroit.

One real and present danger connected with a certain type of brand name is depicted by the cartoonist Keane with the caption: "Tonight's special, 'Why Junior Can't Spell,' was brought to you by the makers of Kwik Koffee, Minit

Pudding, Tastee-Ade, Choc Snax, Froot Bits, Korn Chips, Sweetie Treets, Jelli Muffins and Sooper Soup." Granted that these names are all imaginary, the peril is real. Back in the dim past, an entire row of elementary school spellers went down on "does," which they insisted on spelling D-U-Z.

The public relations field is an integral part of advertising, whether in connection with brand names and products, political parties, or movements and organizations of all kinds. A prominent public relations man warns his fellows to be on guard against the element of distortion. Another admits that the writing is slanted, but adds: "We never lie; we just present the facts." A third man, moving from newspaper work to public relations, was told frankly by a former colleague: "I'd rather you had decided to hand out towels in a Hackensack whorehouse!" An exaggerated view, perhaps, but one that illustrates how public relations and what may be called "huckstetrics" go hand in hand in the popular mind.

Part of the impression is no doubt due to recent disclosures concerning the weasel wording used in packaging products for sale in supermarkets—"large," "jumbo," "mammoth," "colossal," "supercolossal" for olives; "king" and "superking" for cigarettes; "personal," "medium," "regular," "large," "large economy," "family," "giant" for soap products; words that can be stretched to convey all sorts of mistaken impressions. Unit pricing is claimed to be the cure for this evil. We shall see. Other weasel words in marketing are such terms as "on sale," which Bess Myerson Grant has decreed must apply to at least half of the stock under consideration. But then, what is the definition of "on sale"? An elderly lady shopkeeper of my acquaintance used to put on sale, periodically, items that didn't move too well by the simple expedient of pricing them *up* from ninety cents to a dollar, with the "on sale" tag, and claimed the method was extremely successful. All that was needed were the magic words.

The word "save" (you "save" by buying something now —of course, you would save much more by not buying the item at all) is so overused in advertising that it is even satirized on TV, where a giddy wife who comes home with a $300 fur stole explains to her distraught husband that she bought it with money she had "saved" by buying, on the same buying spree, three separate household appliances, each for $100 less than granny had paid for them.

A purely numerical practice for deception, carried over into the present from an earlier day of semiliteracy, is the pricing of goods at something like $39.99 (or even $39.95), instead of a frank and forthright $40.00 (it always goes above $40.00 with sales taxes anyway). Who (or whom) do they think they're kidding?

Then there are such well-chosen terms as "chicken steak," "California roast," "quarter pork loin," and "country-style spareribs," which the New York State Department of Agriculture and Markets recently banned from New York retail stores, to be replaced by the more down-to-earth and less exotic "chuck steak," "chuck roast," "loin pork roast," and just plain "spareribs." Other fanciful innovations marked for extinction are "his and her steak" (anything from a Delmonico to a chuck), "watermelon roast" (rump roast or bottom round), "lollipop steak" (anything from sirloin to chuck).

The Federal Trade Commission labels "puffery" such overenthusiastic phrasing as "best in the world," "the greatest buy in town," "goes like the wind" (this for a motor scooter than can achieve 40 miles an hour), "works to keep you looking better longer," and anything else that cannot legally be proved to be true or untrue, but "sounds very nice." "Puffery" is otherwise defined as "poetic license —embroidery of the truth to give it its best face," "a throwback to the Barnum days," "something that may be accomplished with music, movement, and sex as well as with words," "an expression of opinion not made as a representation of fact." But some puffery is permissible, even by FTC standards—if the claim is obviously absurd, irrelevant, or the exaggeration is trivial, such as "25 percent faster" when it's only 23 percent.

The true stamping ground of modern advertising is not so much the printed word of packaging, newspaper-magazine publicity, and store proclamations of bargains, but those two great audiovisual devices of the last half century: radio and television. The latter, felicitously called "Videot's Delight" by some wit, is probably the worse offender of the two, both because it appeals to two senses instead of one and because it demands the undivided attention of its addict. Both justify their existence with programs that may be good, bad, or indifferent. But their real function is to persuade you to buy, and this all-important message must perforce be carried by a commercial. The art of making good, or at least plausible, commercials has yet to be learned by the advertising agencies. Sponsors should by this time have become aware that no matter how good the programs they sponsor, what they really have at heart stands or falls on their commercials. Hearers and viewers are congenitally heartless ingrates, caring little who brings them their favorite programs. People like me watch such programs without paying the slightest attention to the sponsors—unless, that is, the commercial has the same standard of excellence as the program, which very seldom happens. But we become acutely conscious of commercials that offend us by being loud, vulgar, or stupid. The agencies have sold their clients on the proposition that all that is needed is infinite repetition, that if you can get the people to listen to or view the program they will naturally fall for the product that is dinned into their ears and displayed *ad nauseam* before their eyes. Nothing could be farther from the truth. The truth is that at least as many are turned away from products as are attracted to them by the commercial message.

One is compelled to sympathize with the sellers of certain products which by their very nature are unappetizing and do not lend themselves to glamorization. Such things as mealtime plugs for depilatories, deodorants, mouth washes, acid indigestion pills, or, worse yet, fly killers and remedies for smelly feet simply cannot appeal, and are condemned to waste their sweetness on the desert air. Still, they could be subjected to tests of good taste. There is quite a difference between a cartooned picturization of Raid against the insects and an actual display of one hundred dead roaches. And what is more depressing than Excedrin's skull and crossbones, accompanied by the knell of doom? Or is it meant to induce the headache it is said to cure?

Then there is the little matter of plausibility and logic. Some commercials try to get around this by offering sex. The Simpering Swede urges you to "take it all off!" for instance, or the Finicky Finnette implores you to "put it all on!" The attractive young airline hostess informs you: "I'm Clare! Fly me to Timbuctoo!" which aroused all sorts of dream-visions until David Frost satirized it by having a bearded Castro follower follow three girls, point a gun at the audience, and exclaim in no uncertain terms: "I'm a Fidel man! Fly me to Havana!" and a cartoonist produced a caricature of President Nixon in his characteristic gesture with arms raised, and the caption: "I'm Richard! Fly me to Peking!"

One may substitute drum pounding and the blaring of trumpets for a true sales appeal, like the truculent, over-loud "Coming through!" theme of a certain automobile, or the meaningless, loud-mouth address to his sales force by a head salesman for a soft drink with an unbecoming name that is still trying to make its way east. Some try their hand at humor that elicits a grin the first time you see it but palls on constant repetition ("Sorry, Charlie!" "Say Charlie sent you, forsooth!"). A little bull-throwing is done by the brokerage firm that is "bullish on America."

There are the commercials that insult the viewer's intelligence, whether the viewer be a man or a woman. A women's liberation organization recently came out with a list of the ten commercials most objectionable to their sex. But even before that, one advertising executive had gone to the trouble of conducting a poll among six hundred members of her sex to discover "the ten brands whose advertising women hate most." She came up, among others, with a deodorant described in conversation between two men in adjacent apartments who, by some miraculous misadventure of construction, share the same medicine cabinet; the toothpaste that "gives your mouth sex appeal"; the little kid who interrupts a public gathering to inform his dad that he has only one cavity; the talking dove; the outer-space man who interrupts his stellar trek to advise the woman of the house about a detergent; the "Colorless Twister"; and the "bad breath" sequence. Had the poll been taken among men, it is likely that Josephine the Plumber and Hazel the Maid would have joined the roster. John Beaufort, in the *Christian Science Monitor,* brings up the objections voiced by women's liberation leaders against displaying woman forever in the home, the kitchen, the laundromat, the supermarket, and the drugstore. Also, Mrs. Ohsonicely is portrayed as being glad she's a woman not because of any outstanding achievement, but because of her deodorant. The image of women as "household robots" and "sex symbols" is not merely depicted, but flaunted by the commercial media, the critics charge.

But women are not the only ones who object. One Bill Benson has formed what he calls a "Committee for the Rejection of Obnoxious Commercials" (abbreviated to "CROC"), which proposes to offer each year to ten advertising agencies ten Emmy-like "CROC" awards for the year's ten worst commercials. One news commentator commentated that "one man's CROC may be another man's delight."

There is the "folksy" approach exemplified by "the good folks of Valley Mountain Spring Water," who may be all of that, but are primarily interested in selling you their product; or the spurious camaraderie of "the Dodge Boys"; or "your friendly Junko dealer," who usually is just that, but occasionally turns out to be a sourpuss.

Mottos and slogans are legion. A few are aggressively competitive, running down rival products, like the "Uncola" of which the Colas pretend to take no notice, preferring to wage their own internecine struggle with appeals to a hypothetical "Pepsi Generation," or claims that "It's the real thing!" (Are the others "unreal"?) But whether they are or aren't, we are still puzzled by that song sung by a big mixed choir on an Italian hillside. Which came first, the song or the commercial? Aside from the fact that the song itself is cloyingly sentimental, one wonders whether the overtone inserted by the refrain is meant to convey the suggestion that if all the world would learn to drink the beverage in question, universal peace, love, and harmony would reign.

Even better than having all people learn a common language, no? This observer's reaction is that its opening words should be changed to "I'd like to teach the world to think."

The negativism of the "Uncola" is carried to its outer limits by a commercial for another product that boasts of the fact that it has *no* hydrohexaline, or whatever the chemical is that the competition parades. Is this advertising by subtraction? Or negation?

The agencies are not above plagiarizing from one another's scripts ("You'll find a friend at Banker's Bank," but "You'll find a banker at Truster's Trust"; a third institution describes itself as "a people's bank, helping people grow"). One automobile comes out with "a better idea whose time is here," but its major competitor offers you "an idea you can live with." One margarine product, borrowing from the afternoon soap operas, gives you "the continuing Saga of Harold's Mother."

Few people dislike beer. But beer commercials are something else again. Killer Beer talks about "beer after beer," while another brand boasts about "a two-beer thirst," and a third tells you "it's the beer to have when you're having more than one." Then there is the "natural beer" (are the others "unnatural" or "supernatural"?). One consigns all its competitors to perdition ("When you're out of Blitz, you're out of beer!"); exclusivity is also claimed by the one that tells you that when you've uttered its name, "you've said it all!". And there is the one that combines beer with sex by showing a very sexy female who sings that "my kind of guy—my kind of male" drinks no other brand.

Deodorants, breath-fresheners, toothpastes, and aftershave lotions are among the big offenders. One features a good-looking gal who is said to have "the freshest mouth in town"; but the claim is made by two older women, and you wonder how they would know, unless "fresh" is used in the sense of "impudent." Blisterine has "the taste you love to hate—twice a day," and High Ju-Jutsu warns its male devotees to "be careful how you use it," because it causes erotic convulsions in the opposite sex; while Gas Shave makes her want you to "hold her barber-close."

Best among detergent commercials is the one featuring the ritual invocation to the Great God Nab ("Oh, Nab! We're glad they put sulphuric-hydrochloric acid in you!") Best among airline ads is the one that urges you to "Get out of this World!" Ralph Nader has not yet declared planes "unsafe at any speed."

Before cigarette advertising went off the air we had "What a bad time for a Dent!"; the soul-searching "Decisions, decisions!" that accompanied a difficult choice between high flavor and low tar; the romantic "Together!" that harbingered a cigarette for the two of you; "You can take Sell 'em out of the country, but—"; and the most linguistically controversial ad of all, "Like a cigarette should," later followed by "What do you want, good grammar or good taste?" to which the logical reply was that there was no good reason why you couldn't have both, with "taste" interpreted in both its major meanings. "You've come a short way, Baby, if all you've learned to do is smoke like a chimney!" ran into minor difficulties with women's lib, although it was probably meant to enhance the concept of feminine emancipation from the unreasonable and discriminatory injustice of the old-fashioned male.

Then there are the commercials that leave you in doubt as to the hidden meaning or intentions of the advertiser, like the radio piece about Little Red Riding Hood, riding in an automobile to grandmother's house in the company of a Wolf who runs out of gas. "What shall we do now?" says she in a tone of distress. "I guess—we'll have to put our heads together!" he replies. That's the end of the story. Does it mean what one might think it means? And what sort of way is that to advertise a brand of gasoline? Another ad mentions "Schweppervescence" and tells you the product is made by "Sh-h-h; you know who!" But do you really know? Two radio ads speak of "beautiful downtown Newark" (or Brooklyn), and I've always wondered which came first, the ads or the reference to "beautiful downtown Burbank" that used to be voiced by Ernestine the telephone operator on *Laugh-In* ("downtown" appears also in an ad of a totally religious nature reported in the news and designed to prevent the tearing down of a church: "Keep Christ in downtown Squeedunk!"). Another radio ad tells you "It's worth a trip!" to shop at X and Z, forgetful of the meaning of "trip" in the new language of Youth, where "tripping" means to go on a narcotics binge.

It is a curious fact that occasionally commercial slogans make the grade and really turn into household expressions. This the sponsors do not seem to relish, and the too-successful commercial quickly disappears. It happened to "Mother, I'd rather do it myself!" to "*Mamma mia!* That's a spicy meatball!" and is in the process of happening to "Who made the salad?" "Try it! You'll like it!" and "I can't believe I ate the whole thing."

The charge is often made that the language of commercials corrupts standards of good English. This seems to be only occasionally true, provided we accept colloquial American as good English, and if we bar such minor points of misusage as are exemplified in "the most taken vitamin in the world" and "If you can't trust Prestone, who can you trust?" Years ago there was a Halo commercial that ran "Halo, everybody, Halo!" Today we have "It's Cott to be good" and "Versa-tunatility," along with strange child coinages like "gooky" (seemingly from "gook"—dirt, sludge, slime—reported in Wentworth and Flexner's *Dictionary of Slang* from as far back as 1949 and etymologized by the Random House Dictionary as a combination of "goo" and "muck") and "gnucky" (could this be a borrowing from Italian *gnocchi*, potato-and-flour dumplings?).

Foreign languages are not too often used, and when they are, they are, in the main, well handled. Mothers running after children who fail to brush their teeth yell *"¡Qué no te limpiastes los dientes!" "Reviens! Tu n'as pas brossé!"* and *"Non ti sei spazzolato i denti!"* in authentic Spanish, French, and Italian. But Jean-Pierre Aumont should have his ears pinned back for deliberately mispronouncing his native tongue and, worse yet, encouraging his listeners to do the same. "Zizanie" is zee-za-NEE, not ZEE-za-nee. All he's doing is deferring to the English speaker's tendency to stress the initial rather than the final syllable.

One sage concluded that "advertising is baloney disguised as food for thought." But it's a creative process and opens up fascinating vistas of what one can do by combining a new libretto with existing jingles; for instance:

> Rooster makes beer, and I don't care,
> Rooster makes beer, and I don't care,
> Rooster makes beer, and I don't care,
> Especially for you!
>
> *or*
>
> Yummies are yummier,
> Tummies are tummier,
> Crummies are crummier,
> Hot dogs are doggi-er,
> And coffee is coffee-er!
>
> *or*
>
> The charcoal's in the flavor,
> The flavor's in the filter,

The filter's in the charcoal,
In that good new cigarette!

One final note about radio and TV concerns not the advertising, but the slogans that newscasters and MC's coin for themselves, somewhat like a brand name—a minor form of personal advertising, if you will.

Back in the early days of radio, Gabriel Heatter used to open and/or close his newscasts with the exclamation "Ah! It's bad [or good] news tonight!" uttered in a doleful or joyous tone, as the circumstances might warrant. Another famous old-timer, Walter Winchell, used to start his evening broadcast with a distinctive "Good evening, Mr. and Mrs. America, and all the ships at sea! Let's go to press!" The late much-liked and much-lamented weathercaster Carol Reed used to close her brief programs with "Have a happy!" which, when you first heard it, sounded as though her final words had been chopped off. Huntley and Brinkley's "Good night, Chet!" "Good night, David!" were widely satirized and imitated. Walter Cronkite's closing words embraced a world of philosophy: "And that's the way it is" with the date following. At an earlier period, when he ran the *You Are There* show, he closed his programs with a statement that was less philosophical and accurate and more ambiguous: "What sort of a day was it? A day like all days, filled with the events that alter and illuminate our times!" Roger Grimsby starts with "Hear now the news" and closes with "Hoping your news is good news." John Wingate has a somewhat mysterious invocation to "Great World that you are!"

One WOR newscaster, Lyle Van, got into the habit of saying good-night to his listening children with "Good night, little redheads, and everyone!" This went on and on until the little redheads had acquired little redheads of their own; but when he tried to discontinue it, there were loud protests from his listeners, and the "little redheads" went right back in. Another WOR newscaster and disc jockey, John Gambling, aided and abetted by his second-in-command, Peter Roberts, without actually creating a slogan, has coined a delectable if imaginary word, "grackelry," that spurious branch of zoology that studies the life habits of the grackle, a great and noble bird.

The attitude of program directors toward commercials varies. There is blistering scorn in the way Alfred Hitchcock mouths the word "commercial" as often as it interrupts his program. Others have euphemized the "commercial" into "a message" or "a word from our sponsors." The best is probably Ed Sullivan's announcement of an oncoming commercial as a "sixty-second memo." Another euphemistic gem is Garry Moore's "Let's pause for a moment for a transfusion to our treasury."

A secret ballot on commercials conducted among newscasters and program directors would be infinitely revealing. But don't bank on it. The agencies would never stand for it. Think what it would do to them!

The Phraseology of the Arts

Closest of the arts to the field of commercial advertising, and most subject to its baneful influences, are the performing arts of stage and screen. How the methodology of publicity is applied in weasely fashion was brought out not too long ago by Vincent Canby, motion picture reviewer for *The New York Times.* He was taking exception to an ad published in his own paper on behalf of Ingmar Bergman's film *The Touch,* in which he was quoted as saying that the picture "tells a love story full of the innuendos of his [Bergman's] genius." Since this struck him as cryptic and ambiguous, he looked up what he had actually written in his review. The latter merely said: "Bergman's *Touch* tells a love story"; but then, *ten paragraphs later,* went on to say: "Bergman may occasionally make dull movies—as I believe *The Touch* to be—but he cannot be stupid, and *The Touch* is full of what might be called the innuendos of his genius." Labeling this process "promotion-by-emasculation," Canby cited another sample, in which the ad quoted him as having found the film "truly comic"; what the reviewer had actually said was: "Beatty's gambler-turned-business-man is a truly comic, clay-footed entrepreneur." After objecting to the "hysterical punctuation" that the ad people feel compelled to dress their quotes with, Canby pleads for the Culture of the Big Hustle: when they take something out of context, they should take it out in one unbroken piece.

To take another phase of the same phenomenon, *France-Amérique*'s movie critic protests the use made of the name of Jules Verne to present on Broadway a "revolting blood-and-guts time waster, advertised as 'Jules Verne's *Light at the Edge of the World*,' in which the original *Phare du bout du monde* is submerged in a sea of sex and sadism."

This is what happens on the fringes of what is left of the movie industry. Within that industry itself, there is a proliferation that takes the form of pictures and series of pictures for TV consumption, where they are linked directly to what was previously discussed—the commercials. But the gods of advertising have decreed that there shall be no direct connection or remote resemblance between the program and the commercials that accompany it. Only on rare occasions do we encounter commercials that are not in strident contrast to the program. A thrilling suspense story of spies and saboteurs in action is likely to be punctured by ads for lipsticks, cleansers, detergents, or beauty aids. There is something incongruous about being left hanging from a cliff to be informed of the merits of ladies' wigs, or, conversely, to have a heart-rending soap opera interrupted in the midst of a life-and-death conversation to be told that an airline will whisk you up, up, and away to wherever your heart fancies on fly-now-pay-later terms, and even let you dance in the aisles.

Many motion pictures and pictures made expressly for TV have undeniable merit. Others justify the claim once made about a producer: "He has plenty of taste—all of it bad." My own perverted tastes happen to run to pictures of action: war, spy, detective stories. But I demand that they be plausible. I half enjoyed *Desert Rats* until I began to notice that the aim of the four protagonists was so deadly that they never failed to bring down their opponents, but the aim of their German foemen was so bad that none of the four good guys ever got nicked. Didn't the Wehrmacht teach its men how to shoot before shipping them to North Africa?

One series that goes on forever (probably by reason of its mechanical features), even though its cast keeps on changing, is *Mission Impossible.* But while the gadgetry may be all there, lots of other things are not. Are the foreigners all dopes? Don't they know how to take even elementary security measures? Are there no guards at the border toward which you see the successful team speeding, and no telephones or radio to alert those guards? A black man acting as a driver, mechanic, or repair man in European countries beyond the Iron Curtain would draw plenty of attention, but nobody ever seems to notice his color. (Jan Carew, a black Guayanan, describing in the pages of *The New York Times* his experiences in Eastern Europe, titles his piece: "Being Black in Belorussia is like being from Mars.") Worst of all, the Impossibles seem to speak all languages, and well enough to pass themselves off as natives. In one episode, in a country that was obviously Hungary, they communicated with Hungarian guards, soldiers, and officials by the simple expedient of using English, which all the Hungarians understood and spoke flawlessly even among themselves. Here we have a standard of comparison with an earlier era in picture making in Douglas Fairbanks Jr.'s *Affair of State,* where an artificial "Vos-

nian" language was created and used by all the "Vos-
nians," and which the hero could not speak or understand,
a fact that was vital to the plot.

It has been pointed out that *Hogan's Heroes* (where,
incidentally, all the Germans are unbelievably stupid, from
the lowliest guard to the colonel in charge of the prison
camp) has lasted longer than World War II; but that is
merely a matter of timing and expediency. Why stop if
there is a market for it? It has also been brought out that
the World War II flick *Kelly's Heroes* has one of its characters saying that "he's freaking out," a phrase that wasn't
invented until well into the Vietnam war; but that is a mild
and forgivable anachronism.

In my earlier book, *Words in Sheep's Clothing,* I referred to two of the three awards periodically bestowed
upon actors, actresses, and producers by that great Mutual
Admiration Society which comprises the world of stage,
screen, and television. I overlooked the "Emmy," which
pertains specifically to TV acting and producing, and is
awarded by the Academy of Television Arts and Sciences.
Where and how did the name originate? Webster Third
informs us that it was coined from the name of Faye Emer-
son. The most recent of our sources, the American Heritage Dictionary of 1969, states that it is a variant of
"Immy," an affectionate abbreviation of "Im(age orthicon
tube)." Why the shift from "Immy" to "Emmy"? To make
it sound like a person's name, like its two predecessors? It is
of interest that American Heritage, though it lists "Oscar"
and "Emmy," overlooks "Tony," while Random House, with
"Oscar" and "Tony," forgets about "Emmy." The origin of
"Oscar," which the dictionaries label "obscure," may have
a different story from the one I tentatively advanced in

1969. The new story is that instead of an anonymous secretary saying the statuette looked like her uncle Oscar, it was Bette Davis who said it reminded her of her then husband, whose first name was Oscar. There is one more possibility, but it presents very doubtful features. There is an Australian slang use of "oscar" for money ("I'll bot some oscar from a cobber," translated as "I'll wangle some dough from a sidekick"). This is said to have originated by some sort of rhyming slang from the name of John Oscar Asche, an Australian actor who died in 1936. But would the Australian slang term have penetrated the American screen language? One additional award, which has not yet made it in any dictionary, is "Obie," for "O.B." (Off Broadway) productions.

Among terms that have recently cropped up in the tongue of stage, screen, and TV are "smash flop" (a take-off on "smash hit"), "sinema" (coined by *Variety*), "residuals" (royalties paid to a TV actor for repeated use of the film or commercial in which he appears). TV has developed what it calls a "Première-Encore," for a TV production put on for the second time (what used to be known as a "Repeat"). I was once puzzled as I viewed a "World Première" that I was sure I had seen before; then the little word "Encore" struck my eye.

"Nudie" is a generic name for films that feature nudity, and "tweenies" are the materials shown between the sex scenes in foreign movies. The tweeny-writer is a member of a new profession that puts profundity into the intervals between sex. Anti-American speeches are said to go over big between nude scenes. They are then properly translated for reuse abroad. Philosophically, sex is considered the "tweeny" of life.

Two picturesque terms that have come into usage from Yiddish are "schlock" and "shtick." The first, usually in the form of "schlock product," means a film to be reedited. "Schlock" does not appear in Webster Third, but is given by other sources, both earlier and later. It is defined as inferior, cheap, trashy merchandise, and goes back to Yiddish for "broken," also used in the sense of "curse," which in turn stems from German *Schlag*, a blow. "Shtick," which is so recent that only American Heritage lists it, is defined as a characteristic trait, an individual way of doing things. It goes back, through Yiddish, to Middle High German *stich*, a thrust or puncture. As currently used on the stage, it means that the actor or actress who is given to "shticks" goes beyond the call of duty in expressing individuality.

There are also native coinages and definitions by critics. A *New York Times* reviewer, Antony Newley, describes a new singing voice as "a yowling diphthong bray," and Merv Griffin, speaking of art and music fans, suggests "fannies" as a suitable feminine form.

This section would not be complete without a mention of the famous Voluntary Film Ratings—GP, R, M, X, etc. Jack O'Brian suggests a new rating for disgusting films: IIICCCHHH! Dan Carlinksy, in *The New York Times,* expresses his dissatisfaction with the film rating system and suggests a new and simpler one: S—Sexy; VS—Very Sexy; TS—Too Sexy; NST—foreign film with nudity, but with well-placed subtitles; DTM—children under seventeen admitted, but Don't Tell Mother; VLTV—Violence, but less than on TV; VP—political film approved by the Vice-President; ZZZ—family film. Why not?

In the field of music an amusing "Glossary of the Musical Avant-Garde" is supplied by Donal Henahan in *The New York Times*. Overlooking his humorous and slightly fantastic etymologies, he outlines the recent use of terms borrowed from unrelated fields ("aleatory," "stochastic," "indeterministic," "collage," "happening," and "ploys and gambits" are a few random samples). Others pertain legitimately to the musical field: "Augenmusik," for example, is "music that pleases the eye," further described as "for advanced pupils only"; "dodecaphony" is the "twelve-tone method of composing"; "extended-time music" is based on patterns "sequentially exfoliated to the point of inducing quasi-religious ecstasies," and "silence" is "a parameter that can be organized into a musical composition, formerly called rest." Others are pure but significant spoofs: "Nono" is said to be an Italian twentieth-century composer of leftist leanings whose attacks on the Vietnam war have made him unpopular in the United States, to the point of giving rise to the phrase "That's a Nono." "Stravinskycraft" is said to be a publishing factory based in Hollywood, specializing in scholarly broadsides. Stravinsky himself exemplifies the "game theorist," a composer always willing to play with a new theory when the usefulness of the old one wears out. Imaginary items like "moog" and "orff" are introduced (the second is the bark of rage uttered by avant-garde critics when faced with modern but traditionalist music). Stray slang forms are "pot," claimed to be an electrical engineering term for potentiometer; "white noise" (scientific term for acoustical or electric noise), said to occur when a major symphony orchestra is confronted with the possibility of black membership; and "tape head," one who is high on tape recordings.

Brief definitions of musical forms include "Classic" (soft music with few notes); "Modern" (loud music with many notes and projected slides); "Popular" (not serious); "Romantic" (medium-loud, with fairly high note density); and "Sonata," changed to meet modern requirements by having no subject and, usually, no object. An imaginary

Flemish fourteenth-century musicologist, Antonius Theophrastus Drivel, is given credit for having first used "the conflation of the cadences," "non-continual simultaneities," "parametric structuralism," while Stephen Potter's disciples are blamed for "non-equivalent pitch collections," the "square-tooth wave," "non-random density-weight distribution." Clearly a spoof, but one that points to a trend.

A few redefinitions are in order. "Celebrity," for instance, is redefined by a wag as the advantage of being known by persons who don't know you. Two generic terms that in the view of some are interchangeable are the not so recent "camp" and "kitsch." The former, which does not appear in the artistic sense in such older sources as Oxford and Webster Third, is defined by the ultramodern American Heritage as an affectation of manners and taste considered outlandish, vulgar, and banal. Random House goes further; after defining "camp" as extravagant, artificial, exaggerated, it goes on to establish a cleavage between "high" and "low camp," though the precise difference is not discussed, and even promotes it through functional change to verbal status ("to camp"), which means to act affectedly, often with homosexual overtones. "Kitsch," which surprisingly does not appear in American Heritage, is defined by Webster Third and Random House as art of little value, but of popular appeal. Both derive it from dialectal German *kitschen*, to throw together, to scrape up mud from the streets. Again to our surprise, Webster Third quotes "kitsch" from an author born in 1907, which would seem to indicate that it has been in use for some time. Unfortunately, no time reference is available for "camp" in the artistic sense. Other general uses of the word go back to the sixteenth century, and in the sense of battle, now archaic, it can even be found in Anglo-Saxon, which apparently borrowed it from Latin *campus*. The contemporary connotation was probably coined by Susan Sontag.

Arty language is constantly being coined by the arty. One curious contribution offered by cat fanciers is "cellár cat" (with stress on the second syllable of "cellar") for what used to be commonly known as an "alley cat." Sidney Delevante, winner of the "Art in the Park" festival award in Newark, N.J., states in one of his poems that

> Some artists paint today for todayers,
> Some for tomorrowers . . .
> Some don't and some do
> Have followers.

4

The Rapping of Youth

The younger generation has been described as a group that is alike in many disrespects. Yet, there will always be a youth, if mankind is to go on. Also, if history is any criterion, there will always be a Youth Movement, a militant Younger Generation, bent upon undoing the work of its predecessors and setting up a New World, in which injustices and abuses of all descriptions will be erased, and the Millennium will be ushered in. There will always be the "Cause-of-the-Month" Club. There is, however, consolation in the thought that "the Now Generation will be the Then Generation by the time we get adjusted to it," and that the motto of the Young Rebels, "Never trust anybody over thirty!" carries the seed of the Young Rebels' own undoing.

A new word created by those who specialize in environment demonstrations is "ecolike." Another division of Youthful Reformers, whose bag is surreptitiously cutting down unsightly billboards along our highways, proudly call themselves "Billboard Bandits" and "Midnight Skulkers." They arouse the ire of farmers on whose property the billboards are located, who say that the billboards serve the added purpose of sheltering their cows from the sun. The Billboard Bandits take their justification, if any, from Ladybird Johnson's Highway Beautification Program.

There is vast concern among older writers for the outrages inflicted upon language by the younger generations. David Susskind, who can hardly be accused of overconservatism, came out at the end of 1970 with a protest about the monosyllabic speech of his daughters and their associates, which he described as consisting mainly of such expressions as "Ya know, man," "It's like aaaaa . . .", "It's like heavy, ya know!" "Shouldn't we be teaching them to speak better, to think straighter . . . how to make their points with appropriate English?" he plaintively concluded.

Another writer, Arthur Nader (no relation of Ralph), claims it's impossible to keep up, for purposes of a movie script, with the chatter that pops out of the mouths of hippie characters, who get through a day of talking and never use more than twenty expressions, or maybe a hundred words, repeated endlessly—"man," "bag," "thing," "hangup," "chick," "freak out," "trip," "way out," "wild," "crazy," "groovy," "bread," and the like.

What these and other critics overlook is that the Youth Culture (or "Counterculture," as some have named it), while inarticulate in spots, is also linguistically creative. To them we owe such recent additions to a growing family of "-in" words as "rock-in" (a music festival) and "Zap-in"; the latter comes from the name of the little town of Zap, in North Dakota (population about 300), which was selected, for obscure reasons (perhaps the onomatopoetic ring of its name), as the spot where some 10,000 students converged to drink beer, roister, and otherwise disturb the public peace—a sort of mini-Daytona Beach in a northern setting; it took the National Guard to clear the atmosphere. (Wentworth and Flexner report a slang use of "zap" in the sense of to kill, but describe it as "never common"; while American Heritage, describing the term as slang, defines it as to destroy with a sudden burst of gunfire).

Youth's linguistic creativity, particularly in college circles, is manifested in other ways. Existing words and expressions are given strange and brand-new meanings. Take, for instance, "confrontation," a term borrowed from international relations and meaning "forehead to forehead" (something like former Secretary Rusk's "eyeball to eyeball"). There is a use of "confrontation" by bodily contact groups, but in the parlance of the student rebels, the "confrontation" takes place on the campus, between themselves and the administration, and it is always the latter's forehead that is lowered, at least in the script. There are such transferred meanings as "values," "living and giving," "effective living" (whatever "effective" may be intended to mean in this context), "involvement" (everybody must get wrapped up in the New Thinking), and "meaningful dialogue," in which the professoriat, scared to death and inspired by what might be called the Spirit of Munich, gives in to all the "nonnegotiable" demands (if they are nonnegotiable, what's the point of negotiating?)

Above all, there is "relevancy," of courses and curriculum, of instructional and administrative procedures, of life itself. How do we decide whether something is "relevant"? "Relevancy" and "relevant" go back to 1510, and all our dictionaries define them as "pertaining to the matter in hand." They have no meaning until we define "the matter in hand." Are mathematics, sciences, languages and literatures "relevant" to a college education, or shall we restrict ourselves to Black Studies and Revolutionary Techniques? If all we want is discussion groups to argue vociferously about current problems, why not dispense with the liberal arts college altogether and send both faculties and administrations packing? Is it "relevant" to mention the fact that in the USSR, the only country where the Communist Revolution has been carried through to its logical completion, the schools and universities, after a period of initial confusion, were "restructured" into an altogether traditional frame?

But all these academic digressions and logical weaknesses do not invalidate the fact of youthful linguistic creativity. Additional terms contributed by the academic segment of the Youth Movement are "Flunkenstein" (applicable to a student who consistently fails to make the grade) and the elegant "Fratorities" or "Sorernities," coined to describe the new bisexual student houses where the emancipated sexes study, live, and bed together. A "chipster" is a student addicted to munching potato chips.

The "Hate Generation," consisting of "kids" who are often graduate students well over twenty-one, seems responsible for the current use of the verb "to trash," which means to wreck, burn, or otherwise devastate a university building or other property. This word, whose origin is defined as "obscure" in all our dictionaries, appears as a verb in 1618, but in the meaning of "to hold back or restrain a dog" or, at the most, "to trim dead leaves and branches from a tree." The British Oxford Dictionary further informs us that it appears in 1859 in western U.S. usage with the meaning of "to efface"; this is confirmed by none of our American dictionaries, but might supply a plausible genealogy for its use by rebellious students.

The radical militance of some of the Youthful Hate Groups has led columnist Russell Baker to add a few imaginary movements of his own: "Lout Liberation," aimed at restoring freedom of self-expression to America's louts, long ruthlessly silenced by the codes and standards imposed by the polite Establishment for imperialistic and genocidal reasons; "Grouch Now!" which follows the Misanthrope's Manifesto; "Free Our Necks!" the extremist faction of "Ramfast" ("Radicals and Militants for a Skinnier Tie"); "Scholars for a Simpler Society"; "Sadists' Liberation"; and last but not least, the "Movement for a More Meaningful Movement."

Concerning the more general language of the hippies and those who ape them ("Apies"?), there is the rather recent use of "Street People" to betoken those who in a past era were called bums, hoboes, or vagrants; and "Groupies," who have been likened to medieval camp followers, teen-age girls who try to sleep with as many members of rock groups as possible, and who have a British counterpart in the "Pop-Show Dollies." "Jesus Freaks" (but that's what their enemies call them; their own name for themselves is "Jesus People") are that segment of the youth movement which follows a revivalist trend. Two of their favorite slogans are "Turn on to Jesus!" and "Holy Ghost Power!"

There is the use of such abbreviated forms as "vibes" for vibrations, and "hypo" for hypocrite or hypocrisy; and even an ingenious written or gestured symbol, L + 7, which adds up to a "square" whom you don't want to call that to his face. Let us also recall the definition of parents as "the sum of the squares on the two sides of the family."

There are interesting resurrections of medieval authors to justify current usage: *Saturday Review,* for instance, cites Chaucer's *Canterbury Tales* to the effect that "I wol lette for to do my thynges," while the New Testament is paraphrased in this guise: "If someone socks it to you on the right cheek, let him sock it to you on the left"; and a part of the wedding ceremony comes out in this guise: "Speak now, or forever cool it!" On the other hand, a picturesque sample of ultramodern usage is recorded as follows: "If that's where your head is at, let it be; no use fighting bad vibes; stay loose!" (The last phrase is the new version of the slangy "Take care!") One of the more colorful youthful interjections, abundantly reproduced in commercial advertising along with "Together!" is "Wow!" which is described as originating in Scottish English in 1513, then spreading to America, where in the 1920s it underwent an extensive process of functional change ("She's a wow!"; "We wowed them last night"). The reasons for its popularity as an exclamation of mixed wonder and delight are obscure. The equivalence of "Wow!" to the "Hot dog!" of the 1920s, of "It's groovy!" to "It's the cat's meow!" and of "Scram!" or "Split!" to "Skiddoo!" was recently stressed in connection with the perennial changeability of youthful language.

At airports, the term "skyhitching" has been coined by modern youth to signify thumbing plane rides to your destination, on private planes for the most part, but occasionally even on chartered flights, with the connivance of a member of the crew.

At nudist camps, the term "palechest" has been coined to designate outsiders.

"Bread," commonly used in the hippie culture to signify money, has an interesting variant among Hawaiian hippies: "fish and poi." Then, in the field of real food, there is a scientific-sounding "macrobiotic" diet (one conducive to a long life), which calls for considerable restraints. Backsliding from this somewhat strenuous practice is known as "binging."

The question of timeliness in this language often comes up. James Baldwin, in the course of a TV rap with Margaret Mead, made the point that both the black and the youth languages undergo change, so to speak, under pressure, the necessity of not letting the pigs understand what the adepts are saying. But this may be to some extent an *ex post facto* generalization. Language changes constantly, and the language of some groups is notoriously unstable. The claim is also made that this type of language changes because of overuse in advertising, and that such terms as "groovy," "What's happening?", and "Together!" are now definitely out, while "cat," "cool," "shuck," and "far out" are on their way out. In a comprehensive study in *Time Magazine* for June 6, 1971, Mike Jahn, rock reviewer, consigns to the archaic 1960s such terms as "heavy" (in the sense of powerful), "rap," "stoned" (which has gone on to "high," then to "wrecked"), "bust" (arrest), "cosmic," "where it's at," "trip" (on drugs), "to shtick," "groove on," "hassle," "organic," "out of sight," "put down" (insult), "put on," "strung out" (said to have progressed to "spaced," "wasted," and/or "wrecked"), "Together!" "vibes," "goof on." Standbys that continue in use are "far out," "up," "down," "bummer" (bad experience), "shuck" (a phony), "planet" (earth), "get down," "get it on" (start), "turn his head around" (convince him), "get into." Said to be new expressions are "wasted," "trash," "right on," "brother," "sister," "third world," "people," "pig," "to off" (to kill a pig), "to do a number on someone's head," "to rip off," "to do dope" (any kind, in any way), "ups" (amphetamines), "downs" (barbiturates), "joint" (marijuana cigarette), "smack" (heroin), "toke" (puff), "roach" (butt of a joint), "ripple and reds" (wine and barbiturates), "dude" (guy), "jive" (bullshit), "to truck" (to walk jauntily).

It may be observed that there is only partial agreement among the authorities as to what is truly current, what is obsolescent, what is archaic. In another frame of reference, "busted" (arrested), "hassled" (harassed by police or outsiders), "trashed" (vandalized) are claimed to be quite current in the language of the Street People.

It will also be noted that several of the terms in Jahn's list refer to marijuana or hard narcotics. A study published by the Institute of Mental Health gives the following popular terms for marijuana: "weed," 'hemp," "loco weed," "giggle grass," "LSD," "reefers," "Mary Wanna" (or "Mary Jane"), "Tea Brand Sticks," "boo," "Swinging Mother's Trip Kit." But the trouble is that some of these are trademarks of legitimate cigarette brands as well. There is even one of these named P.O.T., with an asterisk keyed to the words "Plain Old Tobacco." The Mexican *Oro de San Marcos* ("St. Mark's Gold"), a variety of tobacco, has given rise to *Oro de San Andrés* ("St. Andrew's Gold") for marijuana, and this in turn to "Acapulco Gold," used to describe a potent Mexican variety, stronger than the domestic.

Another study, published by the Drug Awareness Committee for the guidance of parents, gives the following popular terms for marijuana: "pot," "grass," "locoweed," "Mary Jane," "Tea," "Gage," "Reefers," "Hashish." Heroin goes by the pseudonyms of "H," "Horse," "Scat," "Junk," "Snow," "Stuff," "Joy," "Powder," "Smack." Morphine takes the forms of "White Stuff," "Miss Emma," "M," "Dreamer"; while codeine is sometimes called "Schoolboy." LSD can take the aliases of "Acid," "Sugar," "Big D," "Cubes," "Trips"; MDT that of "Businessman's High." The amphetamines are known collectively as "Bennies," "Dexies," "Co-pilots," "Wake ups," "Lid Poppers," "Hearts," "Pep Pills"; the methamphetamines may be "Speed" or "Dynamite"; the barbiturates, "Barbs," "Blue Devils," "Candy," "Yellow Jackets," "Phennies," "Peanuts," "Blue Heavens," "Goof Balls," "Downs."

Then there are the organic solvents—airplane glue, gasoline, aerosols, and cleaning fluids—that are inhaled by the use of paper and plastic bags or poured on rags and handkerchiefs (slang terms: "sniffing," "Glue sniffing," "the Bag," "Fluid"), which are devastating in that they cause respiratory depression and possibly brain damage.

Whatever the purely sociological implications of all the foregoing may be, the linguistic indications are clear. The Youth Language, in all its branches, shows abundant signs of both creativity and change. The charge that the younger generation is inarticulate is unwarranted. It finds terms, and plenty of them, for everything it wants to rap about. What it wants to rap about is another matter.

5

Sex Rears Its Ugly(?) Head

Sex is one of the most rewarding fields for the researcher after the new. Whatever some may think, it is fairly obvious that sex is here to stay, both as an institution and as a fount of linguistic creations. Weasely features abound.

The word "sex" itself is a primary source. By reason perhaps of the easy combinations into which the prefix *ex-* enters, columnists and writers seem to revel in creating new "sex-" compounds. The following recent coinages have come to light: "sexational," "sexplicit," "sexplanatory," "sexercises," "sexhibitors," and, with "sex" in the middle, "hobosexual" and "desexgregation" (the last was used as a slogan by the women's liberation demonstrators who invaded the New York Stock Exchange on August 26, 1971, but its opposite, "sexgregation," had been suggested by this writer three years earlier).

From Scandinavia comes the exquisite (or should we say "sexquisite"?) "sexmesse," for a Copenhagen pornographic exhibit, or "sexhibit." Here there is in evidence the influence of the Munich *Buchmesse* (a monster exhibit of books), which in turn was probably coined from the older *Kermesse*, a word of Dutch origin, first appearing in English in 1577, denoting an open-air fair, whose religious background is evident from its parts (*kerk* + *mis*, "Church mass")—a far cry indeed.

Stemming from Greek *porne*, harlot or prostitute, the "porno-" of "pornography" further branches out into "pornovel" and "pornovelist," while pornographic magazines have been telescoped into "pornzines." Other random creations are "eroduction" for erotic production, the name given by the Japanese to low-budget skin-flicks; "smorgasborgy," bearing the Swedish stamp of *smörgåsbord* combined with orgy; and "lewdity," formed on the analogy of nudity.

To these edifying coinages, characteristic of what Bishop Fulton Sheen has labeled the "contraceptive society," may be added "gonocide," for birth control through the male rather than the female organs, and the cute adjective "beddable," for a member of the female sex who is easily led to bed (here there is a minor controversy as to whether the spelling should be "bedable"; but the rules of English syllabification, such as they are, would seem to call for a doubling of the *b*, in addition to which a single *b* might lend itself to confusion with "bedabble"). The word appears in none of our most recent dictionaries, but is logically enough formed on the verb "to bed," which in one of the dictionary definitions is "to have sexual relations with."

Among the more obvious and slangy formations are "horny" (to be sexually aroused), for which no date appears; Oxford does not report it in the wanted sense, though it gives under "horn" the older meaning, still current in the Romance languages, of the emblem of cuck-

oldry; but Wentworth and Flexner, while carefully refrain-
ing from dating it, say its use is uncommon; it is possible
that it has flourished again in the course of the Vietnam
war. There is also an ironical "Penis Power." Among the
more elegant and intellectual forms is "daughter-of-a
bitch," which makes plenty of sense and goes along with
the previously reported "whoreson," resurrected from
Middle English. There are the reversed film titles *I Am
Yellow* (*Curious*) and *I Am Blue* (*Curious*), for which
there is justification in the fact that pornographic films are
known as "blue films" in certain circles. Many were
stumped by the superintellectual and highly recondite title
of the stage production *Oh, Calcutta!* and wondered what
the name of a city in India might have to do with the
subject matter. They were enlightened to the fact that this
was an English-language transcription of a very slangy
French exclamation (*"Oh, quel cul t'as!"*), which we
choose to leave untranslated; after all, there is no reason
why the curious, yellow or blue, should not do some of
their own research.

This use of foreign languages in sexual connections may
be regarded as a form of euphemism, a survival of residual
prudery. There is the use of the French *voyeur* (literally
"viewer") as "Peeping Tom," though it might be objected
that the modern "voyeur" does not peep but pays his good
admission money at the box office. While this term appears
in all our current American dictionaries, it is absent from
the British Oxford, possibly because the French meaning,
extending to "sexual degenerate," is stronger than the English.

Then there is the use by the respectable press not of four-
letter words, still viewed as substandard, though abundantly used in so-called literature and on the stage, but of
highly technical polysyllabic forms in their Latin originals

that send readers scurrying to their unabridged dictionaries, where they invariably appear, again with the partial
exception of the British Oxford. A single issue of *The New
York Times* featured "coitus," "fellatio," and "cunnilingus," the first of which is reported even by Oxford and goes
back to the sixteenth century. Since all are faithfully recorded in our major comprehensive American dictionaries,
there is little point to defining them here. Of greater interest
is the fact that two of them, "coitus" and "cunnilingus," go
back to good Classical Latin, while "fellatio" seems to be
of Low Latin formation (but the doer of the action, *fel-
lator,* and the action itself, *fellare,* both appear in the Classical Latin dictionaries).

There is even the coinage by traditionally minded nuns
of the term "Berrigan's Bunnies," to describe those Sisters
who follow the rebel priests in their philosophy and sport
mod garb; as well as the suggested replacement of the time-
honored term "dirty old men" by "sexy senior citizens,"
offered by Dr. Victor Kassell, a Salt Lake City geriatri-
cian.

Despite all claims of sexual liberation, there is still an
abundance of euphemism and understatement in the field.
A university professor who was discussing certain experiments came out with "pictorial erotic stimuli" to refer to
dirty pictures. "Meaningful relations" is often used to describe sex as well as intellectual and emotional communication; "relate to" may mean to have sexual relations with;
and in experiments similar to the one mentioned above, an
"encounter group" sometimes becomes a plain sex orgy. A
few additions to the lingo of interpersonal relations come
from a fellow who was convinced by friends to try a singles
weekend at the Concord or another hotel in the Borscht
Belt. He coined the expression "meaningful quickie" from

his encounters with women whom he met at the bar, while group confrontations were taking place in adjoining rooms. A week later he coined "coolie quickie," which denotes a meaningful relation (or relationship) at a ski lodge.

The use of "adult" in connection with films, stage productions, books, etc., is often a euphemism for sexy or obscene. What may be viewed by an "adult" audience may not be viewed by children, save perhaps under proper supervision. This brings up an interesting question that is often asked: what etymological or semantic connection, if any, is there between "adult" and "adultery"? Actually, none. "Adult" goes back to Latin *adolescere*, "to grow up," which in turn is formed from *ad,* "toward," and *alere,* "to nourish or to raise" (the same root that gives us the *alma* of "Alma Mater," fostering mother). "To be nourished or raised toward (maturity)" would be the exact meaning of *adolescere,* and an adolescent is one who is undergoing that process, an adult, one who has completed it. "Adultery," with all its derivatives, goes back to Latin *ad alterum,* "to another." *Alterare* is the verb formed from *alter,* and in simple form it gives us "to alter, to turn into something other than what was there originally." In Latin itself, it is compounded with *ad* to form *adulterare,* "to change into, to corrupt," more specifically a woman (*adulterare matronas,* "to commit adultery with married women"). It merely so happens that by the laws of Latin sound-change the *a* of *alere* and that of *alterum,* when compounded with a preceding preposition, turn into *u,* giving "adult" and "adultery" a resemblance that is striking, even though stray.

Another set of expressions that show strong, although logical, semantic progression, is the one that comes from "swing," both verb and noun. This word, of Anglo-Saxon origin, takes full flight in Middle English with all of its conventional physical meanings. In the 1930s the name is bestowed upon a type of jazz music with a compulsive rhythm, and even becomes the name of a dance (however, "Swing Waltz" had appeared earlier, with the literal meaning of swinging your partner). From this point, "swing," "swinging," "swinger," begin to assume more sexual aspects. Random House describes "swing" as a modern, lively, knowledgeable attitude, and a "swinger" as a lively, active, modern person. American Heritage defines "to swing" as to participate actively in youthful fads. Wentworth and Flexner give one slang acceptance of "swinging" as hip, in rapport with modern attitudes, and even cite a Frank Sinatra album of 1956 entitled *Songs for Swinging Lovers*. Beyond this, all is silence; but current usage has carried on "swing" to the concept of accepted and mutual infidelity, with "swing parties" where husbands and wives are interchanged. The password for this type of entertainment is said to be "Let me show you the house," an invitation to a guest of the opposite sex to retire with the host or hostess to a bedroom where the Exchange (or "Sexchange," if you prefer) functions in full.

Edifying or not as these practices may be, it is undeniable that the use of euphemisms in the language of sex goes very far back in history. Even Victorian English established in 1844, according to Oxford, the use of "to service" in the sense of "to cover a female animal," as a bull "servicing" a cow. On the purely linguistic score, we have no ground for complaint.

Homosexuality has recently come out in the open. Unofficial statistics place the number of homosexuals in New York City at between 500,000 and 800,000, with 20 to 30 million across the nation. There have been many demonstrations by a "Gay Liberation Front," which demands for its members the right to behave as they please without concealment. The term "gay" itself, however, referring to a homosexual of either gender, calls for clarification.

The trouble is that "gay" is hard to fix in time. While homosexual practices go back to the dawn of history (one need only refer to the Biblical Sodom and the personal habits of Socrates, Sappho, and other ancient Greeks of renown), the word "gay," first appearing in Middle English, into which it came from Old French, Old Provençal, and eventually a hypothetical Gothic *gaheis*, which has an attested cognate in Old High German *gāhi* ("sudden," "impetuous"), does not seem to take on any immoral connotation until 1475, when it is used as a noun and applied to a "gay lady" or to a "gallant" (but "gay lady" is undefined, and "gallant" is a lady's man). This use quickly died out, but the word was revived to describe one of "immoral life," not further qualified, in 1637. Wentworth and Flexner, in 1960, record "gay" in the sense of homosexual; so do subsequent dictionaries, though most of them attach the label "slang" to it. One strange digression is reported by Oxford for 1802, when "gay" was applied to a woman as a term of praise. We are all familiar with such expressions as "gay bachelor" and "gay old dog," but there is no precise indication of homosexuality in Oxford, which nevertheless gives us a U.S. slang usage from 1899 in the sense of "forward," "impudent," "fresh." All this would seem to indicate that the specific use of "gay" as homosexual arose in the late 1950s, between the Oxford 1955 revision and the 1960 Wentworth and Flexner *Dictionary of Slang*. The indications, however, could be misleading, by reason of Oxford's occasional reticence in connection with U.S. slang (Oxford does, however, report "queer" in the sense of homosexual). The use of "gay cat" to refer to one who is inexperienced seems totally unconnected, though the two slang meanings of "gay" must at times prove confusing. But that's the way slang works. On the other hand, the organized homosexuals have recently expressed a desire to give up the designation "gay" in favor of "herosexual." There is some doubt as to whether the general public will accept this halo of heroism in connection with homosexuality.

6

The Paean of the
Liberated Woman

It is unfair to pin the label of "desex" or "unsex" on the women's liberation movement, as some have done. At no time, to our knowledge, has the movement advocated the drastic ancient remedy invoked by Lysistrata. But women's liberation, which has many facets, holds, among many other things, that there is overemphasis on sex so far as women are concerned. The glamorization of woman as a sex object, the stress placed by our affluent society upon the purely sexual function of woman, whether blatantly exposed in sex films, sex advertising, beauty contests, or thinly disguised by presenting woman's role in society as primarily that of a mistress, wife, or mother, are those aspects of modern society which women's liberation deplores.

But there are other and more important aspects to the movement. There is the question of women's right to act as free agents, untrammeled by traditional shackles; to follow careers and occupy posts for which they are fitted; to receive equal compensation for equal work. Should not women themselves be the arbiters of whether they shall bear children, and how many they shall bear? "The only good abortion law is no abortion law" is one of the mottos the movement flaunts. This runs counter to the principle that it is ethically wrong to destroy human life, even in embryonic state. How to reconcile the two principles, both of which seem justified on ethical grounds?

In the matter of employment, women's liberation points to the fact that while millions of women are employed, they are often discriminated against when it comes to top jobs and fattest salaries. With nearly thirty million women in the labor force, the average female, white or black, earns 60 percent of what the male earns, according to official census figures, or less than the average black male, who in turn earns less than the average white male. For this, there is ancient Biblical precedent. The Old Testament book of Leviticus prescribes fifty shekels of silver for a male to thirty for a female. The number of women occupying posts of top responsibility in business and industry is pitifully small. There is a constitutional provision barring discrimination of sex in both employment and promotion, but the courts often adopt what has come to be known as the "B.F.O.Q." ("bona fide occupational qualification") exception, based in turn on the unofficial "sex plus" theory, to the effect that while a woman cannot be barred because of her sex, she can be barred because of her sex plus one additional factor—age, weight, marital status, parental responsibilities, and so forth. This brings up the question, Can a company refuse to hire the mother of small children when it does not bar the father of the same small children? Issues of pregnancy, physical strength, and the nature of the occupation (custodian of a men's lavatory in a hotel or restaurant, for instance; though women often occupy such posts in European countries) enter the picture. There is also the factor of "role differentiation"; only about 46 percent of occupations employing over 100,000 persons of both sexes have as many as 35,000 of each sex. The question arises, Could not more women fulfill more masculine roles in large segments of occupational categories, as they do, for instance, in the Soviet Union?

The movement complains that far too few women occupy political posts, appointive or elective. Yet women do occupy such posts, and perform in them certainly as satisfactorily as do their male colleagues. Thus far in this country, no women politicians have been accused of graft. Also, a recent Gallup Poll indicates that voters of both sexes, by a two-to-one margin, are willing to vote for a qualified woman candidate for President of the United States. This is a spectacular reversal of a similar poll held in the 1930s, when two out of three voters declared their unwillingness to accept a qualified woman. It is more than likely that in the political field, as well as the economic, inequalities will gradually be ironed out.

This leaves two angles of the women's liberation movement out in the open, both of which present dubious as well as humorous features, and it is here that the play of weasel words takes on importance.

The first is the natural reluctance of a great many women to abandon their present status, which has advantages as well as disadvantages. Legally, socially, and domestically, women have enjoyed many traditional privileges of their sex. Columnist Ernest Cuneo points to what he calls the "Sisterhood of the Wedding Ring," jealous of the prerogatives with which they are endowed by virtue of a contract that is both social and legal. Many are reluctant, in extreme cases, to give up the institution of alimony, designed to provide for a divorced wife who may have means of sustenance superior to her former partner's. Hand in hand with this go those practices which need not be gone into save by referring to a couple of weasely expressions, such as "Golddiggers" and "Diamonds are a girl's best friend." Socially, there is a reluctance to give up those amenities whereby men have traditionally deferred to women, from tipping their hats and giving up a subway seat to the "Women and children first!" of the lifeboats when a ship is sinking. In the home, there is considerable evidence that most men shoulder their fair share of the burden, in addition to fulfilling their traditional role of providers. Under the circumstances, it is not surprising that there should have arisen countermovements to women's liberation, exemplified by HOW (Happiness of Womanhood), whose heraldic device is a pillow, symbolical of the sheltered life under male protection, or, better yet, the "Pussycat League," which holds that women should continue to pursue the role of small, cuddly, pampered pets, at least where possible. (The "Pussycats" have devised the term "Nasties" for militant women's libbers.) Overall, there is the unspoken fear of the deglamorization of woman, of her loss of desirability in the precise function to which women's liberation objects—as a sex object.

The other and more serious angle is imbedded in some of the connections, avowed or implied, of women's liberation with other movements, not merely that of legitimate civil and human rights for racial minorities, but those that seek not to reform, but to subvert, by all manner of means, direct and indirect, violent and nonviolent, what the majority regard as the established order of our society, which despite all imperfections has within itself the possibility of orderly and peaceful change and improvement, unlike certain other highly touted societies where true repression is the normal way of life, and the individual is not free to express dissent or opposition, under penalties that may reach the point of extinction.

The women's liberation movement is not a single organization, but a group of loosely federated associations, ranging from NOW (National Organization for Women), founded in 1966 by Betty Friedan, and said to have over 120 chapters distributed over the nation, to something picturesquely but disturbingly describing itself as SCUM ("Society for Cutting Up Men"), whose precise extent and aims are, luckily perhaps, not available to us.

We have before us two interesting publications, one of which, entitled *Off Our Backs,* is published occasionally by "a group of women in Washington." The issue under consideration is Summer 1971. Some of the items are fairly factual and enlightening. "Dr. Jekyll and Your Hide," for instance, is an account of harrowing experiences undergone by women in connection with abortions and medical examinations. Another, "Dig Yourself," is an anatomical discussion of the female body, in popular, practical, and extremely frank terms. Then there is an account of the practice of medicine in what our official circles now describe as the People's Republic of China. In connection with the problem of overpopulation, one article entitled "Who Says Too Many?" presents the case for further expansion of the world's population, contrary to the current trend toward population control, and is, in a way, a curious duplication of the stand of the Roman Catholic Church in relation to that problem. There are such features as "The Return of Chicken Lady," "Priceless Survival," and "Culture Vulture," and a slogan appears, "Don't Forget to Smash the State!" which sounds like the SDS Manifesto.

On the purely linguistic side, we find the use of "women's

priorities" and "women's participation," "sex category," and "sex discrimination," and even "sexism" and "sexist," formed on the analogy of "racism" and "racist" (these forms appear in none of our major dictionaries, and must be described as innovations). We also find "elitism," which appears in some American dictionaries, though not in Oxford, with the meaning of belief in the rule of an elite; "ego trip," another innovation. "Pushy" and "unfeminine" are said to be adjectives constantly on the lips of those who do not approve of the women's liberation principles. Issue is taken with one of the dictionary definitions of "menopause" as change of life. "Why 'change of life'?" inquires *Off Our Backs;* "All life changes!" "Sisters" is used for members of the movement, and two prefixes, *co-* and *vice-,* are condemned as being too often applied to women whom the dominant sex wishes to relegate to a place of inferiority ("co-chairman," "vice-president").

A distinction is made, as indeed it should be, between "suffragist" and "suffragette," though both are derived from Latin *suffragium,* "vote." "Suffragist," first appearing in English in 1822 to denote an advocate of the extension of the political franchise, was stretched in 1885 to cover an advocate of votes for women; its Greek suffix, *-ist,* is noncommittal as to sex and merely indicates the follower of an *-ism.* "Suffragette," first recorded in 1906, is specifically feminine with its French ending *-ette,* and is defined by Oxford as having violent or militant overtones. It was probably meant to be disparaging at the time it was coined. Another interesting term is "masculine mystique," used to betoken that set of traditional beliefs whereby the male is the superior creature. The word "mystique," borrowed from French and first appearing in English in the early 1950s, stems from an original Greek *mystos,* which in turn comes from the verb *myein,* to initiate into religious rites. It is described in the dictionaries as a complex of beliefs and attitudes centering about a person, institution, or idea—a credo, a cult, a guide to action, surrounded by an aura of mystery. It would be hard to convince most men that they are that good.

The other document under consideration is the *International Women's Calendar* for 1971, copiously illustrated, and published by the All-Women Collective of Sisters, though with acknowledgments to Brothers as well. Among the Sisters' groups mentioned are the "Redstockings," and we wonder whether this is a take-off on the English "Bluestockings," or the French *Bas Bleus*. The motto is "Women of the World, Unite!" and Mae West is quoted to the effect that "marriage is for the women who fail in every other way."

A few divergent spellings appear in the *Calendar* which may or may not be significant of liberation from spelling conventions: "advertizing," "Facism," "Bolshevick." There is the use of one slangy expression in "expose the Women's Rights Bill for the shuck it is before a Senate Committee." "Shuck," a word of uncertain origin, normally means "husk" or "pod"; as a verb, "to remove the husk, usually from corn." Oxford records also a dialectal and U.S. usage dating back to 1847 as something of little value, while Wentworth and Flexner define a slang use as "fake," first recorded in 1957, with "shucking" translated as "bluffing" or "faking."

Beyond that, the *Calendar*'s illustrations portray such curious and meaningful episodes as the one from 1621, when "one widow and eleven maides" were transported to Virginia from London and sold for 120 pounds of tobacco each; and in more recent times, the 1969 episode of Grinnell College students who disrupted the address of a *Play-*

boy representative by disrobing in protest over the commercialization of sex, thus making the punishment fit the crime. The beheading of Anne Boleyn is presented, in close proximity to the organization of the American Red Cross by Clara Barton and the crowning of Queen Elizabeth II.

The roster of women immortalized in the *Calendar* runs from Elizabeth Barrett Browning to Elizabeth Gurney Flynn; from Emma Goldman to Molly Pitcher; from Lucy Parsons, who advocated the murder of the rich by tramps, California Manson style, to Louisa May Alcott and Jenny Lind; from Janis Joplin, who "could not survive being the contemporary sex object of the hip culture," to Mary Baker Eddy, Emily Dickinson, Jane Austen, George Eliot, and Mme de Stael. Historically, we go from Joan of Arc, through Calamity Jane and Carrie Nation, to Margaret Chase Smith and Margaret Mead. It is perhaps too much to expect, in a calendar that calls for precise dates, references to Judith, Esther, the Queen of Sheba, and Semiramis. The roster includes Spain's La Pasionaria, but not Argentina's Evita Perón; Dorothy Day, but not Vivian Kellems; Amelia Bloomer, but not Martha Mitchell. Omitted is even our most colorful Congresswoman, Bella Abzug ("Big Bella" in the words of her political opponents), who in addition to wanting to liberate New York City from New York State also wants to obliterate the distinction in title between married and unmarried women by replacing "Mrs." and "Miss" with an indeterminate "Mis" or "Miz" ("Ms." in writing), to which one commentator remarked that it might be simpler to abolish all "polite" handles, including "Mr.," and just address a person by his or her first or last name. To this, people who have to write and address many letters will utter a resounding "Amen!" (or—as suggested in the great demonstration of August, 1971, in feminist Jacqueline Michot Ceballos's new, revised version of the Lord's

Prayer, "Mater Nostra," which was read on the steps of St.
Patrick's [St. Patricia's, if you will] Cathedral in New York,
of which the full text appears below—"A-women!").

Our Mother who art in heaven,
Sister I call Thy name.
Our time has come,
Our will be done,
On earth, and it will be heaven.

Give us the right to earn our daily bread
And forgive us our trespasses
As we forgive men who trespass
Against us.
And lead us not into subservience,
But deliver us from Adam,
For thine is the freedom and the
Power and the glory
Forever.
In the name of the Mother, and of the Daughter, and of the
  holy Grandmother,
Awomen.

It may be added that the wording of the new prayer has an
ancestry supplied many years ago by Mrs. Mary Baker
Eddy, founder of Christian Science, in her *Science and
Health with Key to the Scriptures,* where Mrs. Eddy gives a
spiritual interpretation of the Lord's Prayer which begins:
"Our Father which art in heaven—Our Father-Mother
God, all harmonious."

"Trust in God—She will provide" and "In Goddess we
trust" are other theological suggestions advanced by members of women's liberation.

The women's liberation objected strenuously to the
newscasters' references to the "Women's Lib Gals" but

made no suggestion as to a suitable replacement. Similar unqualified objections were entered to Norman Mailer's use of "ladies." As reported by Israel Shenker in *The New York Times,* however, plenty of other suggestions are advocated in other connections, particularly by Varda One, publisher of a Los Angeles underground newspaper called *Everywoman,* whose shattering attacks on a language called "Manglish" include advocacy of "Person," abbreviated in writing to "Pn.," which at one stroke does away with the opposition between "Mrs." and "Miss," with Bella Abzug's "Ms.," and even with "Mr." A chairman or chairwoman then becomes a "chairperson," and "Pn." will prefix such liberated names as Betsy Warrior, Ann Fury, and Dair Struggle. Pn. Varda One would also drop "husband" and "wife" in favor of "partner," lump "he" or "she," "his" or "hers," "him" or "her" into "ve" (nominative), "vis" (possessive), "ver" (objective), as in "A teacher must learn to listen. Ve must respect vis students' opinions. They must be important to ver." Lastly, she would proscribe such terms for nagging women as "beldame," "fishwife," "henpecker," "shrew," "virago," and complement "penis envy" with "womb envy." The suffix *-stress* of "mistress," "postmistress," "headmistress," the *-ess* of "poetess," "authoress," even "Negress" and "Jewess," are frowned upon. So are such verbs as "to man" ("How can a woman MAN the barricades?" asks another Liberation journal).

Others object to offensive terms such as "harlot," "whore," "wench," and, on the other side of the distaff, "homosexual," generally preempted by men, with "lesbian" reserved for women. Other objections are to "girl Friday" and "career girl," "man alive" (why not "woman alive"?), "Oh, boy!" (why not "Oh, girl!"?), "Harvard man," but "Radcliffe girl." Still another objection is to the suffix *-son* in family names, such as "Lucy Johnson." Are the objectors aware that the Scandinavian languages make provision for both sexes in patronymic forms, though this usage is slightly archaic: "Olaf Einarsson," but "Kristin Lavransdatter"? Note also English "Nelson" (Nell's son), "Babson" (Barbara's son), etc., which are matronymics, as well as Italian family names like "di Maria" and "di Giovanna."

Another Liberation writer, Mary Orovan, suggests "co" to replace "he" or "she," "him" or "her," with "cos" as the possessive, and even "coself" for "him/herself"; while Dana Densome, in the Boston *The Female State,* feels that since "he" is included in "she," and "man" in "woman," the feminine forms be generalized.

With tongue in cheek, *New York Times* columnist Russell Baker offers his own suggested replacements for current titles: "Murm," abbreviated to "Mrm.," for a married man; "Smur," abbreviated to "Smr.," for a bachelor. Women could then hold their heads high, on a plane of perfect equality, while retaining their "Mrs." and "Miss," he claims.

Gloria Steinem, who is described by Jack O'Brian as "the only chic Women's Lip," is approvingly, even admiringly, featured by Anita de Calers in a French-language article appearing in the January 29, 1972, issue of *France-Amérique,* New York's French-language weekly. Mlle de Calers claims that "a new vocabulary has been created by the American disciples of Simone de Beauvoir," which is a gentle reminder that the women's liberation movement had non-American precursors. Among the terms she cites are "sexism," "male chauvinist pig," "sex object," and "Ms."

To these, the interesting "role reversal" might have been added. This designates the inverted role of a wife who goes out to earn the family's living, while hubby attends to the household chores and changes diapers.

Add also, from the Miami Democratic Convention of

1972, the non-committal "chairperson" and "chairpeople," designed to replace an insufficient "chairman" and an awkward "chairwoman." I might suggest for both these terms the abbreviation "C.P." (or "Seepee"), on the analogy of "M.C." ("Emcee") and "C.B." ("Seabee"). One might even use functional change and speak of "Seepeeing" a meeting.

Pn. Varda One is reported to be preparing a *Dictionary of Sexism,* to which we look forward with interest. Meanwhile, to cover the general situation resulting from the ancient but ever-recurring War Between the Sexes, there is a quote from Damon Runyon that may be worth considering, if not following: "Man's only weapon against a woman is his hat. He should grab it—and run!"

7

The Coin of the Columnists

The language of reporters and columnists continues to be one of the more fruitful sources of additions to our and other tongues. The journalist is in close touch with current events and changing history. When he is faced with a new situation, or a new angle on an old situation, it is only natural that he will either manufacture his own words or combine existing words into new ones that will convey the exact shade of meaning he wants. Some of them may turn out to have weasely features by their implications, like the "Pentagon Papers," which by a process of association already fostered by the news media evoke in the mind of the reader a whole sequel of happenings, real or fancied (very much fancied, in the case of the "Buckley Reconstructions"). Other combinations are both fortuitous and fortunate, like Roche's "political amnesia," which duplicated an earlier "moral amnesia" in formation, but reminds us that the masses tend to forget both campaign pledges and previous experience with them. We have even the coinage of mottos, like "Make love, not buttons," that satirizes a well-known youthful slogan, or ironical definitions, like that of "fame" as the advantage of being known by people who don't know you.

There are such columnistic creations as "wife transplant," borrowed from the medical field of heart and kidney transplants, and used to betoken a divorce followed by a new marriage. For a certain type of international relations, there is "Finlandization," which indicates a peaceful economic take-over of a small nation by a big one, as of Finland by the USSR. This readily lends itself to such extensions as "Czechoslovakization," for a take-over by a display of overwhelming force, or even "Hungarization," for a take-over by the actual use of such force.

Two extremely fruitful combination words for the journalists are "explosion" and "gap," previously reported on at some length in a previous volume, *Words in Sheep's Clothing*. What goes on in our colleges and universities has been characterized as "Youth Explosion," with the footnote that this may be only too literal in some instances. But the news media speak with evident self-satisfaction of our "information explosion," which occasionally assumes the aspects of a "misinformation explosion," and of the "communications explosion" that somehow forever seems to fail in its purpose. The "gap" previously attached to "generation," "missile," and "credibility" has recently multiplied with a "management gap" (as in the case of Lockheed and Penn Central); a "technology gap," once descriptive of the superiority that America boasted over the rest of the world, but which now is said to be rapidly closing as Japan, West Germany, and other nations cease to look to us for scientific improvements and sometimes manage to surpass us; and even a humorous "therapy gap" applied by one of the columnists to the unsuccessful aspects of President Nixon's attempts to cure the many diseases of our Sick Society.

In a satiric article in the *Christian Science Monitor* (August 26, 1971), Melvin Maddocks coins the expression "Youth Explainers" to define people like Margaret Mead, Charles Reich, and the late Paul Goodman, who tour the "Carson-Cavett-Frost circuit" to present the "youth problem" and the "youth crisis" to the general public, and cites authors and lecturers with the alliterative names of Kenneth Keniston and Erik Erikson to the effect that this segment of the Counterculture is inspired by "cruel zealotry" and "messianic self-righteousness."

So much for the ingeniously creative aspects of the journalistic language. There are some negative features, however, which leave you in doubt as to whether they are deliberate and tongue-in-cheek or due to the accident of ignorance.

There seems to be no valid excuse for "a social criteria" and "an alumni," or for "a more fuller understanding" (*Newark Star-Ledger* editorial, February 23, 1972). No less a writer than Bishop Fulton Sheen writes "Who are you going to live with?" There are such misspellings as "phosphorous" for the noun "phosphorus," Jack Anderson's "concensus," and others such as "irresistable," "indispensible," "tax deductable," "compatability," "inadmissable," and "vaccilate," which shows influence from "vaccinate." What of "substantive," so often used for "substantial?" "Substantive" is legitimate enough, but in adjective use should mean independent, real, and not "in considerable amount." There is a use of downright wrong words, as when an editorial about indictments speaks of "the lengthy proceedings that mitigate against the defendant," where it was obviously the editor's intention to say "militate."

The journalistic mind is much given to telescoped forms and the creation of what Lewis Carroll called "portmanteau words." For the most part, these are deliberate, and clearly due to a somewhat weasely desire to be cute and draw attention and admiration. Occasionally they leave you in doubt, like the "attrified" which seems to combine "attrition" with "atrophied." "Thumbsuck" is a journalistic term used to denote a news story that will not be offensive to the authorities of the country from which the reporter reports, like some (by no means all) correspondences from Moscow, Peking, or Saigon. It is clearly derived from the infant's habit of sucking his thumb and thereby becoming pacified, and the dictionaries present "thumbsucker" and "thumbsucking," though not the usage here described. Columnist Jack O'Brian, one of the major geniuses in the field of Carrollisms, and a worthy successor to Walter Winchell and Louis Sobol, supplies us with the following list: "thighscraper" (for miniskirt); "belly-dancerie" (a place where the *danse du ventre* is featured); "pleasuresque," "tripewriter," "legislady," "schooligans," "geriatricksters" (somewhat ungallantly used in reference to Ann Corio), "saloonatic," "doomwhimperer," "aginner" and "aginnism," "snarlathon," "filmosque," "millionheiress," "chutzpatic," "best smeller," and, with a touch of French, "entrechatting." He resurrects Winchell's 1945 "woofled" (drunk) and "blessed event," which he describes as of long standing, but now on everyone's lips. Speaking of the book *Our Gang,* he coins the elegant "portnoyance." In another column, he offers "to hoist the grunt" in the sense of "to pick up the check" (Wentworth and Flexner have "pick up the grunt," which they attribute to Westbrook Pegler in 1951, in the sense of "foot the bill," but "hoist" seems to be O'Brian's personal contribution). "To take a leave of abstinence" has also been reported.

The *Hollywood Reporter,* with its flair for the flamboyant, has a headline "Hix Nix X Pix," which translated means that farm-belt dwellers reject X-rated movies. "Politigabble" is Russell Baker's own coinage, offered in his *Poor Russell's Almanac.* "Codel" was coined by Drew Pearson to designate a Congressional delegation on a junket. "Ameritocracy" seems to be the creation of John Roche. Other random contributions are "commyrot" for Communist propaganda, "nexterday" for tomorrow, "birthquake" for the former "population explosion," "Splitsville" for the situation where a couple are about to enter the state of holy divorce, "Glamorabbit" for Playboy Bunny, "povertycrats" for those in charge of poverty programs (and "povertycats" for the victims of the programs), "trendency," "chargealcoholic" (a tippler with credit cards), "televisionary," "microemotivism," "gapster," "conglomerateurs" and "rapee" (those who form conglomerates, and the victim of a rape, both with an elegant French nuance), "apparatchik" (here the touch is Russian, and the reference is to a member of the Communist *apparat,* or political espionage machine; but both "apparat" and "apparatchik" seem resurrected from an earlier day, perhaps the McCarthy era, as they both appear in Webster Third).

There is little doubt that all analogical coinages dealing with the deterioration of New York City are of journalistic origin. They include "Times Scare," "Slime Square," "Crime Square," and a "Gun City," which is obviously based on Mayor Lindsay's "Fun City."

To "put in a plugola" for somebody is obviously based on the earlier "payola." The suffix *-ola* is described by Wentworth and Flexner as of Italian origin, but the other dictionaries prefer to derive the suffix from "Victrola" (whose records were among the first to pay off).

There is little point to deploring the excesses of the journalistic language. In the main, they do not debase the language, but add to it an element of inventiveness which at the least imparts a picturesque though fleeting touch. At the most the new words have a chance of becoming permanent and gaining widespread acceptance, terminating in that final accolade: admission to the dictionaries.

8

Pedagese, Psychese, Scientese

It has long been known that there is a brand of language that is peculiar to educational circles. In its lower reaches, it is characterized by circumlocution and euphemism, as when a secretary becomes an "administrative aid," and a truant officer an "attendance teacher," or "visiting teacher." There are meaningful phrases that express more than they seem to on the surface. As brought out by the author of *Up the Down Staircase,* Bel Kaufman, "Let it be a challenge to you" means "You're stuck with it"; "It has come to my attention" means "You're in trouble"; "interpersonal relationships" is translated as a fight between kids; and "ancillary civic agencies for supportive discipline" is, in effect, "Call the cops!"

The tangible result of this soul-searching process after the proper form of expression comes out in letters of appreciation from students, of which a typical one begins:

"You're the only English teacher that ever learned me English real good."

The phraseology of Pedagese includes such choice terms as "peer group," "established society," "participatory democracy," "social skills," "meaningful role," adding up to a "moral imperative to improve the quality of life today."

In its higher reaches, the "multiversity" (or "pluriversity," as Bishop Fulton Sheen prefers to call it) has gone on to such terms as "open enrollment," the consequence of a forcefully expressed demand that a certain proportion of admissions to certain colleges and universities be reserved for racial minorities regardless of previous preparation or the ability to profit by the instruction. This is the reverse of the old *numerus clausus,* which used to prevail in the universities of some eastern European countries down to World War I. The *numerus clausus* is defined by Webster Third as the maximal percentage of applicants of a given race admissible to academic institutions. It was used in Tsarist Russia and Hapsburg Austria-Hungary to keep the Jews from sending to the universities numbers of students out of proportion to their numerical percentage in the total population. Modern America is now bringing back into vogue this old, illiberal, undemocratic quota system based on race rather than merit, which the liberals of an earlier era loudly deplored (in justice to our modern liberals it must be said that a good many of them have come out against it, too). But then America is also the country which in a not too distant past set up discriminatory "ethnical-origins" quotas for immigrants from European countries, with even separate quotas for "North" and "South" Italians, with the border between the two drawn at the line of the River Po.

There are humorous coinages, too, in the multiversity language, such as the "no-time syndrome," said to affect professors who can't take time to explain things to their students, and the "ivory foxholes" into which professors retreat when beset by violence. "Perishable publishing" is Professor Gay Wilson Alden's description of the mania of some academicians for writing textbooks, often "quickie anthologies," which they expect will take the place of original research in their *dossiers* submitted for promotions.

One authentic gem of academic gobbledegook emanating from a great university runs as follows: "The functional methodology shall be based on an inter-disciplinary process model, which employs a lateral feed-back syndrome across a sanction-constituency interface, coupled with a circular-spiral recapitulatory function for variable-flux accommodation and policy modification."

At times, gobbledegook crosses the border from Pedagese into the business world. "Referencing" (meaning "with reference to") appears in a business letter stemming from American Brands dated May 4, 1972.

At both higher and lower levels, Pedagese merges almost insensibly into the jargon of the psychologists. Specifically Pedagese-Psychese are "core concept," "track record," "in-depth resources analysis," "insightful conclusions," "reality therapy." "Mirror image" has been coined for the compulsion of youth not merely to oppose, but to do the reverse of what the older generation Establishment does. "Juvenilize" is the term used for inducing or prolonging childish behavior in an adult, while "graymail," coined on the analogy of "blackmail," is summarized by psychiatry professor Ray Birdwhistell as based on the principle "I will do something bad to you if you do something bad to me"—an attitude, he claims, that is prevalent in millions of families.

For what popular writers call "Body Language," the experts in the field of kinesics use more complicated terms:

Raymond Birdwhistell and Albert Shefler prefer "communication," Adam Kendon "visible behavior," Erving Goffman "face-to-face interaction."

One psychological euphemism that may be said to have an educational aspect of sorts is "street orientation," which means housebreaking for dogs. "Curb your dog" is the more popular version.

The field of science is an area of legitimate coinages, for as science marches on, so does its terminology. What is surprising is that occasionally that terminology breaks out into discussions meant for the layman. Dr. Frank Field, in one of his weathercasts, came out with the expression "Fujiwara effect," evidently a term used by meteorologists. All that resulted from a search of our comprehensive dictionaries and encyclopedias was that Fujiwara was the name of an influential medieval Japanese family, whose members were prominent in politics and the arts. What their contribution to meteorology may be is still, at least to me, a matter of conjecture.

Scientists are sometimes blamed for complicating the language with such expressions as "aerodynamic personnel decelerator" for what is basically a parachute, "metal cylinder storage container" for a tin can, "food service operation" for a restaurant. But these innovations smack of Federalese or Pentagonese rather than of Scientese. On the other hand, it is no doubt the medical profession, abetted perhaps by advertising agencies, that has added "Medic-Home," "Medicenters," "Medicorps" and "Extendicare" to the already numerous family of "Medicare," "Medicaid," "Medical," etc. And there is the recent and weasely "pregnancy interruption" for what used to be an abortion.

The "New Mathematics," which is now the vogue in our school systems, high and low, has led to the introduction of terms that would never have been recognized by the mathematicians of the past: "base ten," "base five," "sets," "groups," "axiomatic systems," "number lines," "associative and distributive properties," "infinite divisibility," "decimal forms of rationals and irrationals."

The computer field, one of the most recent arrivals on the scientific scene, is giving an excellent account of itself in the lexicons and outside of them. Here we have such expressions as "data bank," "machineable records," "turnaround documents," "inputs to the system," "computer systems analyst." These at least sound legitimate to the layman, though he may be powerless to define them with any degree of precision. The most up-to-date of our dictionaries, American Heritage, records none of them, though it does define most of their component parts (not, however, "machineable" and "turnaround").

But then there are other creations that smack of the pseudoscientific and weasely. "Zodiatronics" is the "science" of casting horoscopes by computer, and *Datamation* is the title of a magazine devoted to computer dating. More, far more along this line may be expected.

Another comparatively recent arrival in the scientific field is space, with its language and its slang. In a comprehensive article in the *Los Angeles Times,* Nicholas C. Chriss offers an extended sampling. Some of the words pre-existed the Apollos: for instance, "reticle" (literally, small net; in use since 1731 to describe a network of wires or threads used in the sights of a telescope) and "hypergolic" (self-igniting; from Greek *hyper,* "over," and *ergon,* "strength"). We suspect that "unsymmetrical dimethyl hydrazine" (a component of rocket fuel) belongs to this category, though the dictionaries only give the component parts.

Others are recombinations of old words, but with new meanings pertinent to space: "aeropause," the level above the earth's surface where the atmosphere becomes ineffective for human functions and fades off into space (it appears in the more recent Random House and American Heritage, but not in the older Webster Third or Oxford); "aerothermodynamic border," where the atmosphere becomes too thin to generate much heat; "aerothermodynamic" appears in the older Webster Third, but not in the newer American Heritage; "anomalistic period," the time between a spacecraft's arrival at perigee in one orbit and perigee on the next; and "specific impulse," an expression of the performance limit of rocket propellants arrived at by dividing the thrust in pounds by the weight flow rate in pounds per second. If this sounds a bit confusing to you, take comfort; it sounds that way to us, too.

There are, as one might expect, plenty of acronymic abbreviations: "RGA" for "rate gyro assembly"; "ROM" for "rough order of magnitude"; "PSI" for "pound per square inch"; "POO" for "program zero-zero"; "BURP" for "backup rate of pitch"; "ACE" for "attitude control electronics." There are a few initial-syllable abbreviations of the more conventional type: "sep" for "separation," "rev" for "revolution." There are a few German expressions (after all, the Germans were the first to develop the rocket as an instrument of warfare): *Gegenschein* (literally, "against-light," for faint light area in the sky) and *Brennschluss* (literally, "burn-end," for the end of rocket firing).

In space talk, a rocket engine doesn't fire; it "burns." An "afterbody" is a companion body that trails a spacecraft in orbit (anything from a discarded clamp ring to a spent launch vehicle stage, Mr. Chriss explains). You don't say something is going right; you say it's "nominal." If it's going wrong, you call it an "anomaly." You don't don your spacesuit; you put on a "pressure garment assembly." You don't follow someone; you "configure" him.

Anything weasely about this type of language? Hardly. But it certainly qualifies as professional jargon, which mixes up the layman albeit unintentionally.

⑨

The Language of Law
and Government

While the legal language goes back mainly to medieval Latin and Old French, it also lends itself to new formations which occasionally show weasely features. There is, for example, the very recent California innovation, under a 1970 Family Law Act, whereby the word "divorce" was abolished and replaced with "dissolution" (more easily granted, incidentally, than were the old-style divorces). There are various laws, particularly in New York, designed to protect the consumer from the rapacity of both producers and sellers of goods, and to frown upon such shoddy, tasteless, and irresponsible advertising as is betokened by what a writer on the laws regarding deceptive practices calls "sucker signals": "Buy now or lose the chance"; "You have been specially selected"; "It's only a legal form"; "Just a few easy lessons"; "You can save up to—"; "Yours absolutely free." "Consumerism," an expression that appears in none of our dictionaries, though "consumer" goes back to 1535 and "consume" to even earlier, has appeared as an all-embracing term to cover the protection of consumers. Semihumorous legal coinages have been devised, such as the "commuter neurosis" actually used in suing the Long Island Railroad for damages to the psyche of one of its riders.

The Supreme Court in particular has given us novel interpretations of an old phrase, "conscientious objector." Here there is no question as to the meaning (one who objects to military service on moral or religious grounds), but only as to its application. The latest ruling is to the effect that in order to claim the title, a conscientious objector must be opposed to all forms of warfare, not left free to select which wars he chooses to fight in.

In the matter of the Supreme Court itself, there is a usage of the word "constructionist," frequently applied to the more conservative recently appointed justices, which appears erroneous, or at least incomplete. All dictionaries, including even the British Oxford, which sets the first appearance of the term in 1844 and states that it is most frequently applied to interpretations of the American Constitution, are agreed that the term means one who interprets the Constitution or other laws in a given, specified way, which may be strict and narrow, in accordance with the letter of the law, or loose and broad, with reference to what Webster Third calls "implied powers." It is therefore not enough to call Justices Burger and Blackmun "constructionists"; "strict constructionists" is the proper description. As for the "implied powers," they are best exemplified by some of the decisions of the old Warren Court, which read into the Constitution far more than was there, as when it was decided that a state that set residence requirements for welfare was trampling on the right of American citizens to travel freely, a point that is even now under consideration with a view to revision.

Occasionally the legal language resurrects an older term that has gone out of use and puts it back into circulation. *Quo warranto*, which goes back to 1535 and for which the word "formerly" appears in most dictionary definitions, is (or was) in England a King's Bench writ ordering a person to show his authority for exercising a given office or franchise. Random House informs us that it is also used in the United States, which would make its use not quite so antiquated as other sources seem to imply. The term, incidentally, is to a linguist a horripilating hybrid, using an English term like "warrant" with a Latin ablative ending and combining it with a Latin interrogative pronoun. Its meaning is "by what authority?"

Another linguistic-political archaism is supplied by New Jersey's "Freeholders" (chosen county officials), a term that goes back to early colonial days, when a "free hold" (land that you owned) entitled you to vote. There is a movement to change this title to "county commissioners," in the same fashion in which their Alabama counterparts, formerly called "Ordinaries," were turned into "probate judges," and in Louisiana to "police jurors." But tradition is strong, and the title "Freeholder" stands.

Lastly, there is a new legal concept introduced by economist Ezra Mishan, "amenity rights," which he claims should share equal status in law and custom with property rights, with which they often conflict. "Amenity rights" would presumably be the rights people have in preserving the beauty of their surroundings, as against the property right which would be exercised by an industrial group that had purchased a tract of land in otherwise unspoiled surroundings to erect an ugly, smoke-belching factory on that land that would ruin the "amenity" of the area and the disposition of the dwellers therein.

The language of government and administration falls under two separate headings: that which government itself creates, through the administration, the bureaucracy, or the elected representatives of the people, and that which is created for it and foisted upon it from the outside, most often by the news media. Typical of the former are expressions like "Parochiaid," coined by the Michigan state legislature on the analogy of such existing forms as "Medicaid," "Urbanaid," "Localaid," to describe a form of financial aid to be given to parochial schools in order to enable them to continue their functions. "Lulu," based on "in lieu of," is a flat sum paid to New York State and City legislators and public officials "in lieu of expenses" (it was here remarked that the New York State legislature, in the same breath in which it voted down larger pensions for city workers, voted itself an additional $2,000 a year "Lulu"). "Memcon" is a bureaucratic term telescoped from "memorandum of a conversation." Some doubt attaches to "philanthropoid," an adviser on philanthropy either to government or foundations; "demute," said to be a bureaucratic term for turning up the volume of a recording device; and especially two terms that were in vogue during the Johnson Era to betoken attempts by the Chief Executive to hold both prices and wages under control without actually controlling them: "grandstanding" and "jawboning." The former appears in most of our dictionaries in the sense of playing to an audience, trying to impress the onlookers, or plain showing off, but is not precisely defined in any political sense; it is of interest, incidentally, that not only the verb "to grandstand" but even the noun fails to appear in the British Oxford. "Jawbone," on the other hand, while it fails to appear save as a noun in its literal use, which began in 1489, is given by Wentworth and Flexner as pure slang in the sense of to talk convincingly for the purpose of obtaining credit or a loan, and even to buy on credit. American Heritage, most recent of our dictionaries, offers the meaning "credit" for "jawbone," but only in noun function. It is fairly evident that Lyndon Johnson's jawboning never did get into the dictionaries, and one wonders whether it actually derives from the slang use described by Wentworth and Flexner or is separately formed from the Biblical precedent of hitting people with the jawbone of an ass. The term appears in William Safire's 1972 revision of the *New Dictionary of Politics*. He describes it as originating with Walter Heller's 1962 "jawbone method," used to describe price-wage guidelines, but as having degenerated by 1965 to signify ineffective protest against guideline violations. The journalists have nicknamed Nixon's continuation of Johnson's price-wage policy the "open-mouth policy," on the ground that whereas Johnson's jawboning exerted pressure and voiced opinion, Nixon said nothing. But this is not strictly accurate. There was in the long Nixon Era that preceded the great price-wage freeze of August 1971 an "incomes policy" for price-wage guidelines. The trouble was that it was never applied. Nor does it appear in any dictionary, though "income" is traced back to Middle English. But there is a newspaper definition (see page 139).

Individual creations by politicians abound. Mayor John Lindsay, for example, described a "peril point," which the city of New York had reached and which could be staved off only by copious injections of federal and state aid. "Candidate credibility" was coined by Senator Eugene McCarthy, who is himself nothing if not credible; he is also responsible for redefining Nixon's "Vietnamization" policy as "changing the color of the bodies." "Credibility ·block-

buster," applied to the ill-fated Supersonic Transport Plane
(the SST), was the creation of its chief opponent and nem-
esis, Senator William Proxmire. Attorney General Mitchell
calls his bodyguard a "security coordinator," which is
bound to enhance the bodyguard's prestige. Urbanologist
Moynihan was the resurrector of the phrase "benign neglect," to be applied to overloud racial minorities; Moynihan
himself admits that the phrase originated in 1839, when the
Earl of Durham recommended self-government for the British colony of Canada, which had grown self-reliant
"through many years of benign neglect by the British." But
these expressions tend to proliferate as well as spread. Ad-
mitting his indebtedness to Moynihan's formula, Vice-
President Agnew, on TV, spoke of his own "benign scru-
tiny" of the antiadministration press, which had had, he
averred, the wholesome effect of keeping it within the
bounds of both veracity and propriety.

"Compassionate," immortalized by Senator Muskie and
previously reported, is legitimate enough, going back to
1587 in its generally accepted meaning of suffering with,
sympathizing with, having pity upon. The British have been
using it since World War II in the phrase "compassionate
leave," a leave granted to a member of the armed forces
because of urgent family reasons (one irrepressible British
wit, however, transformed it into "passionate leave"). The
word has now become a shibboleth of the moderate left,
implying that we must view certain sociological problems
with sympathy rather than with Moynihan's "benign neglect," and certain forms of misbehavior with tolerance and
understanding rather than with ire. The word now shows up
even in the speeches of the moderate right.

One of the best sources of neologisms is the Chief Executive himself. It is not certain whether "New Federalism"
originated with him, but there is no doubt about "inflation

alert," "workfare" (this is the President's substitute for public welfare, designed to bring to a victorious conclusion the
war on poverty, hunger, and crime), "governess government" (the overshadowing of the states by the all-powerful
federal establishment, which doles out its bounty to the de-
serving in the form of grants with strings attached, and for
which the replacement would be stringless "revenue sharing"). The "Spirits" of former days, such as that of Camp
David of Eisenhower memory and that of Glasboro fostered
by Johnson, have been replaced in the Nixon Era by the
"Spirit of Apollo." The phrase "let me make one thing perfectly clear" has become proverbial.

Some doubt attaches to President Nixon's actual creation
of "game plan," said to have originated with the President's
love of football, and then been extended to the political
sphere; as well as to "Phase One," "Phase Two," etc., of
the war on inflation, which some columnists claim is reminiscent of the Five-and-Ten-Year Plans of Communist
countries.

But there is more. If an unnamed White House source is
to be believed, Nixon's speech writers have been definitely
instructed to favor certain words and expressions ("time
frame," "firm up," "options," "restructure," "input," "delivery systems," "overpromise") and avoid others ("sce-
nario," "hegemony," "viable," "exacerbate," "meaningful,"
"relevant"). The reason? According to the informant, the
latter words "are among the vogue expressions of the so-
called 'intellectual set,' and have taken on trite and preten-
tious stature."

The federal government alone is responsible for our international relations, and, it may be added, it is quite jealous of that prerogative. Certain innovations seem definitely
connected with our State Department. There is one usage,

however, that apparently got its start in the Department of Defense but has since spread out. "Acceptable" is in Pentagon parlance applied to casualties or damage inflicted by the enemy which still leave us standing (see Chapter 11). Now it has gone on to contaminate the environment (as in "acceptable air pollution") and the economic field ("acceptable unemployment," which in the concept of the administration is what the country can take without too much harm to its economy). The trouble with this use of the term is that it is far too subjective: What is "acceptable unemployment" to a Washington bureaucrat concerned with statistics may not be at all "acceptable" to the man who is thrown out of his job and has a family to support.

Another recent usage is that of "high" and "low profile" to refer to an attitude taken by a country or an administration: we are urged, for instance, to assume a fairly high profile in the eastern Mediterranean and the defense of Israel, but a low profile when it comes to the Far East and the Indian Ocean. But recently even our main international high profile has been lowered, to the point where some speak of a "vanishing silhouette," betokening what others, paraphrasing Senator Fulbright, call the "Impotence of Power." William Safire, in his revised *Language of Politics,* explains this use of "profile" as borrowed from the military: a tank or ship that stands high will draw fire; one that stands low will not.

"Developing nations" is another weasel term that tends to displace older and franker terms ("underdeveloped," "have-not," even "haveless") to refer to those countries that call for the customary economic tribute from both us and our enemies. Like the earlier "emergent" or "emerging nations," it sounds like an overoptimistic projection into the future, somewhat like New York City's "Human Resources Administration."

"People" and "popular," "democracy" and "democratic," are terms of universal appeal, even to those who don't believe in them. There are "Christian Democratic" and "Social Democratic" parties all over the world ("Socialism" and "Socialistic" are less appealing, save to the left wing; yet it is well to remember that the Nazi party was merely a telescoping of "National Socialist"). Hence it is not too surprising that Communist dictatorships adorn themselves with the label of "People's Republics" or even "People's Democratic Republics." The big innovation comes when our own Democratic (or Republican) leaders subscribe to those titles. "Red Russia" was replaced a long time ago by "USSR" or "Soviet Union" in official and unofficial acceptance. More lately, under the influence of what the press describes as "Ping-Pong Diplomacy," there have been other startling changes, in both attitude and nomenclature.

A forerunner of the change was, perhaps, a long article that appeared in *The New York Times* a couple of years ago about the possible significance of the official transliteration of Chairman Mao's name into Roman characters ("Mao Tsetung" instead of "Mao Tse-tung"), but the results were inconclusive. One possible translation was the appellation "Benefactor of the East," but this would come out with or without the hyphen.

After the great Ping-Pong tournament in Peking in which American contestants participated, it was noted that at a banquet given in Washington in honor of Rumanian Premier Ceausescu, President Nixon spoke not of "Communist" or "Red China," or even of "Mainland China," but of the "People's Republic of China." This use of the official Communist Chinese designation for the land that has 800 million inhabitants to the 14 million of Nationalist China (Republic of China) was a harbinger of changed relations. Words can be, and often are, symbolic. Meanwhile, an ironical take-off on the widely touted "two-China policy" is columnist Mary McGrory's "one and a half China policy," the half being, presumably, Chiang's Nationalist establishment on the island of Taiwan, or Formosa. ("Chow Mein Diplomacy" is another coinage by the same columnist).

Interestingly, an almost perfect precedent for "Ping-Pong Diplomacy" is reproduced in the medical periodical *MD* for April 1972, p. 135, from the British magazine *Punch,* which in a 1901 cartoon shows Britannia and China playing Ping-Pong on a table labeled "Diplomacy."

As for the features of obscurity that attended some of the preliminary negotiations leading to the Great Change in our China policy, McGeorge Bundy may be quoted (out of context, since his statement was made in 1963 with reference to our Vietnam policy) to the effect that "a communiqué should say nothing in such a way as to fool the press without deceiving them." Previously, "case of terminological inexactitude" had been reported as the proper diplomatic translation of "lying statement."

The Vietnam peace negotiations in Paris, where some months were initially spent in discussing the shape and function of the table at which the negotiators would sit, elicited a long and subtly ironical article by H. F. Ellis in *The New Yorker.* The author described an imaginary exhibition of antique conference tables to be held at an equally imaginary art gallery in the spring of 2169. Among his creations were the "Winged Circle," putting the table on the agenda rather than the agenda on the table; the "Greek Cross," designed to seat such participants as Israel and Saudi Arabia at the maximum distance apart, yet in positions of perfect equality; and Chamfort's "Triple Decker," with seating layers that would accommodate all Latin American, all Afro-Asian, and all other countries in such fashion that they would be within shouting distance of each other, yet not in physical contact. The author further informed his readers that all these devices became obsolete when it was proposed and carried that all negotiators sit on the ground, country picnic fashion.

The most fruitful field of government innovations is, of course, the tongue of the bureaucratic world, concerning which many volumes have been written. The British, who are plagued by it as much as we are, call it Officialese. In America it goes by several names: Federalese, Federal Prose, Gobbledegook, Bafflegab. "Dictocrats" and "futurologists" are among terms coined (one by Omar V. Garrison, the other by the National Industrial Conference Board) for those who indulge in such language.

Eric Sevareid, in one of his televised commentaries, defined "Gobbledegook" as the normal language of the bureaucrats, adding that "Bafflegab" was used when things got serious. We have tried in vain to find justification for this distinction. But other interesting distinctions have come to light as a result of our search. "Gobbledegook," which has a variant with *y* preferred by some dictionaries, was the 1944 creation of Maury Maverick. Even the British Oxford carries it, though it labels it U.S. slang. It is variously defined as long, pompous, vague, involved language, or wordy, unintelligible, unclear, verbose, bureaucratic jargon. "Bafflegab," on the other hand, appears in none of the major comprehensive dictionaries, from Oxford to American Heritage. It is given only in Wentworth and Flexner's *Dictionary of Slang,* which describes it as the 1952 creation of Milton Smith, a lawyer connected with the U.S. Chamber of Commerce. Ambiguity, verbosity, and incomprehensibility are its outstanding characteristics. One is forced to wonder at this difference of treatment. Why should "Bafflegab" be an orphan in the linguistic world, while "Gobbledegook" meets full acceptance? But there is nothing in the descriptions of either to justify Eric Sevareid's distinction.

Whichever way you want to label it, samples of the bureaucratic language abound; also samples of the mental confusion to which it gives rise. The chairman of the Federal Reserve Board, for instance, is credited with advocating "disinflation without deflation." Again the distinction is far from clear. "Deflation," apparently, first went on record in 1919, while "disinflation" appeared in 1947. Both are described as the opposite or reverse of inflation; both are applied to the price level. Just what did the chairman have in mind?'

Another instance of confusion is reported by Jack Anderson, who states that a public health service grant for "a survey of commercialized prostitution" was listed by the bureaucrats under the heading of "U.S. Government Procurement."

Representative Richard Poff, of Virginia, reports in the *Richmond Times-Dispatch* unearthing a series of choice samples, such as the Defense Department's "combat emplacement evacuator" for shovel, and the Bureau of Public Roads' "impact attenuation devices" for oil drums placed around highway obstructions. High waves causing trouble to shipping are known to the navy as "climatic disturbances at the air-sea interface." A "federally impacted area" is one where there are too many nontaxable federal installations, which reduces the taxable base for the local government and causes it financial distress. "Internal papers" are the "contingency plans" that were so abundantly described in the Ellsberg–*New York Times* revelations, and, according to Secretary Rogers, if any outsiders, or the public at large, find out what is in them, their usefulness is destroyed. Considering the nature of the "revelations," this brings to mind a couple of spurious gobbledegook definitions offered by a columnist: "confidential" is what has appeared in this morning's paper; "secret" is what appeared in yesterday's. More seriously speaking, the security classification "eyes only," which I reported as doubtful in *Words in Sheep's Clothing*, is now given the stamp of authenticity in instructions issued by Dr. John Hannah, AID administrator, and reported as follows by columnist Jack Anderson: "The reproduction of the State's NODIS, EXIS, and TOP SE-CRET and the AID's EYES ONLY and TOP SECRET messages requires the approval of the AID's executive secretary, and such reproduction can be accomplished only by the EXSEC staff. . . ."

In a later column Anderson reports two more authentic terms for the classification of secret documents: "secret sensitive" and "noform" (the latter is a telescoping of "no foreign dissemination").

Another columnist offers a piece of consoling moral advice: "Be thankful you don't get all the government you pay for!"

10

Taxing Words

Talleyrand, one of France's greatest statesmen and diplomats (but also one of history's most famous turncoats and opportunists), is credited with the saying, "The art of politics is to find new names for institutions which, under old names, have become odious to the people."

Mussolini, another statesman who was less of a diplomat, found himself faced with a controversy as to whether certain new forms of taxation should go under the heading of *tassa* or *imposta,* and pronounced: "The economists are not yet agreed as to what is a tax and what is an impost; but the taxpayer at the window finds that it is a futile discussion, because, impost or tax, he has to pay it."

The purpose of taxation throughout history has been to support the existing government and its institutions. As Will Rogers said, "We have the best Congress that money can buy."

The terminology of taxation varies from period to period

and from country to country. What does not vary is the institution itself. "Inevitable, like death and taxes" is another American saying.

The oldest form of taxation on record is the tithe system on the produce of the land. It amounted to one-fifth of whatever was produced in the Egypt of the Pharaohs, two-tenths in the Palestine of the early Hebrews, one-fourth in King Asoka's ancient India. But India also supplies us with a parallel in nature for the institution of taxation, the banyan tree that sends out shoots that take root until a single tree produces an entire forest under which an army can take shelter. Not even death, whose universality and inevitability are linked with those of taxes, has escaped the watchful eye of the taxing authorities. There have been legal taxes on births, marriages, and burials; on windows, doors, and wheels of vehicles; on foreign imports and domestically produced goods; on incomes, inheritances, and legal documents; on wine, salt, tobacco, and slaves; on the use of bridges, roads, and portages; on the privilege of voting and the mere fact of being alive. Taxes have historically been payable in produce, goods, military and menial services, metallic currency, paper money, checks, even credit cards. They have been imposed not only on members of a faith, race, or group that did not happen to be predominant and was generally descriminated against but also on members of the favored faith, race, or group, by virtue of its predominance, which entailed special obligations. Because of the absolute priority of taxes over all other obligations, they have occasionally been compared to the somewhat hypothetical "right of the first night" of the Middle Ages— that is, the lord's claim to the right of the first night with the serf's bride—recently brought into the spotlight by Charlton Heston's picture *The War Lord*. Yet it might be argued that some forms of taxation are self-imposed. When the "numbers" racket flourished in New York, it was euphemistically known as the "voluntary tax." The State Lottery that has now replaced it has been in operation in many countries of Europe for a long time, and there it is known as the "tax on fools," though it might more accurately be described as a "tax on human greed."

The ancient Greeks were the first to introduce a complex system of taxation of which we have fairly complete accounts. Their *eisphora* (literally, "inbringing," "gathering in"), first mentioned in 428 B.C., bore close resemblance to an income tax, imposed upon both citizens and resident aliens. Though it was described as a levy on capital, the capital itself was fixed at twelve times the individual's annual income, which the individual had to estimate and report himself. In addition, the wealthier taxpayers were organized into groups called *symmoriai* (companies), each of which was called upon to raise money for extraordinary expenditures. The wealthier members of the "taxpaying companies" could pay in advance for the rest, and be later reimbursed by their less affluent "partners." Then there was the *telos* (the word that gives rise to our "toll"), which was used at various times as a poll tax on foreigners, as a customs duty, or as a general property tax. *Eponia* ("upon what is bought") was a market tax similar to our excise or sales tax. *Phoros* ("bringing," "that which is brought in") was a tribute paid by satellite states to the ruling state. Two forms of taxation for which there seems to be no modern parallel were the *leitourgia* (public service at one's own cost; the word eventually gives rise to our "liturgy"), which was the obligation imposed upon selected citizens to supply equipment for games, and the *trierarchia* (the fitting of a trireme), a similar obligation to supply equipment for war

vessels. The Greeks seemingly shied away from the direct
real estate tax, imposed on lands and buildings. There is a
Greek term, *ateleia,* that means "tax exemption"; the records indicate, however, that it was very sparingly used.

The Romans, the most methodical people of the ancient
world, were the ones who systematized taxation over a 700-
year period, perfecting it as they went along (or so they
thought), and ultimately making it somewhat like what it is
today. The word "tax" itself comes from their language.
Taxare is a frequentative form of *tangere,* "to touch, han-
dle," later "to estimate, appraise," even "to reproach," as
when one is taxed with a crime or dereliction. From the
semimythical times of the Roman kings who antedated the
Republic there were such terms as *tributum* (our "tribute"), stemming from *tribus,* "tribe," but more literally "by
threes." Ever since the days of Romulus, the population of
Rome had been divided into three groups, and *in tribus
convocare* meant "to call out the entire population in three
groups, or tribes." Each *tribus* was supposed to carry its
weight in supporting the state, and by all accounts they did.
Then there was the *portorium,* a customs duty on imports
and even on some exports. *Vectigalia* was the general name
for the revenues the state derived from its lands, forests, and
rivers, leasing out the lands for agriculture and pasture, and
issuing licenses to hunt, fish, and cut wood; bridge and road
tolls were included. The word *vectigalia* comes from
vehere, "to carry," like the Greek *phoros,* "that which is
carried in to the state."

The national treasury was called *aerarium;* this comes
from *aes,* which is a generic term for most metals, particularly the bronze that went into lesser coins. Among the
things that went into the *aerarium* were gold ingots, remi-

niscent of Fort Knox, which represented mostly the income derived from the manumission tax, a tax paid every time a slave was given his freedom. The *aerarium militare* was a soldiers' pension fund, built up mainly from the inheritance tax. There was even an *aerarium sanctius,* "holier treasury," a big reserve fund to be used only in emergencies, which was built up out of war booty. While the Republic lasted, the *aerarium* was the sole Treasury Department. But with the coming of the emperors, another treasury grew up side by side with it, the *fiscus.* This was the emperor's private treasury, consisting of the revenues of the imperial provinces (as these grew in number and extent, the *fiscus* took the upper hand over the old *aerarium*), as well as unclaimed estates and confiscations, a word that comes directly from *fiscus* and means "something taken into or made part of the *fiscus.*" The word *fiscus,* which also gives us "fiscal," at first meant "light wicker basket," used for carrying olives, figs, and grapes, later used as a money-purse— the emperor's own little Tammany tin box, as it were.

The institution of the *fiscus,* like many other imperial institutions, was retained by the northern barbarians who invaded the Roman Empire. In the seventh and eighth centuries, the Merovingian and Carolingian kings of France still had their *fiscus,* to which they prefixed the word *sacer,* "holy," perhaps as a reminiscence of the earlier *aeramen sanctius,* "holier treasury." The term, it seems, came to be used ironically by the people; instead of "holy tax bureau," it got to mean "damned tax bureau." The word *sacré,* literally "sacred" or "holy," is used today in slangy French with the meaning of "damned" (*Ces sacrés gosses!*—"Those damned kids!"). French is the only Romance language that combines the meanings "sacred" and "damned" into one word, and for this linguistic phenomenon the responsibility probably lies with the "holy" tax bureau of Pepin and Charlemagne.

Back in Roman times, the fact that the emperor's treasury got all confiscated property led to a perceptible widening of the *proscriptio* (our "proscription"), the sale at auction of the property of those condemned, usually to death. After all, it would have been a pity to let their holdings go to waste!

Among Roman forms of taxation whose names have come down to our times is the *decuma* (literally "tenth"; "tithe" is its Anglo-Saxon equivalent). The Latin *decuma* goes on to Old French *disme,* and this, brought to England by the Normans, ultimately becomes our "dime" (one-tenth of our basic unit of currency, the dollar). Normally, the tithe was one-tenth of the produce of the land; if it was paid in cash instead of produce, it was known as *stipendia,* which becomes our "stipend." *Scriptura* was the rental paid for the use of state pastures; this is the same word as our "scripture," but since *scriptura* in origin means a "writing," it is easy to see how the two meanings developed. The Romans had sales taxes, particularly on auctions and the sale of slaves. They had an inheritance tax that ran up to 10 percent on all bequests of over $4,000 to others than those next of kin. Periodically, the value of privately owned land was reassessed for tax purposes, and this was called *indictio,* a word mentioned in the Vulgate. In later imperial times, the Greek *telos,* tax in general, was reproduced in Latin as *teloneum,* or *toloneum,* applied to a toll booth or customs house, and this gives rise to our "toll" and the German *Zoll.*

All these combined forms of taxation occasionally proved insufficient to provide the funds for social improvements deemed desirable by the politicians of the Republic.

Caius Sempronius Gracchus, a member of a wealthy Roman family of rabble-rousers, induced the Senate to approve in 123 B.C. a *Lex Frumentaria* ("Grain Law") providing that wheat be sold at half the market price to all residents of the city of Rome. This was a bit like the over-generous welfare provisions of some of our larger cities; it led to a tremendous influx to the metropolis of people who found life on the farms too barren. The tax system became more and more complex. It bore down most heavily on the rural dwellers who had formed the backbone of Rome's armies, and on the outlying provinces, left to the tender mercies of imperial governors who ground out of the provincials everything that was needed for imperial luxuries and big-city largesses. There were drastic but ineffectual reforms. Tax gathering in the provinces was taken out of the hands of the governors and farmed out to *publicani,* publicans, or private tax gatherers, who even formed stock companies to ply their profitable trade. The publicans, individually or as corporations, undertook to supply fixed amounts of revenue to the central government, in return for which they were granted the support of the military in collecting taxes from the local populations. What they collected over and above what they paid in to the government they got to keep. The result, as might have been expected, was widespread tax-gouging and dissatisfaction, followed by a further exodus from the rural areas and the provinces to the big cities, where instead of tax obligations there were free handouts (*panem et circenses,* "bread and circus games"). Ultimately, a population of urban loafers on relief proved no match for the hardy invaders from the north, and the empire collapsed. The term "publican," incidentally, comes from *publicatio,* "making something public"; this is our "publication," but was also used at the time in the sense

of "confiscation" (posting up the names of tax delin-
quents).

There was, as with the Greeks, tax exemption for a
chosen few. The term was *immunis tributorum,* "immune
from tributes or taxes." Again, the term appears only occasionally in our records.

The Roman system of universal taxation by a central
authority fell apart with the barbarian invasions, though
many of the terms remained. Germanic chieftains imposed
upon their followers and the subject populations payments
that were often capricious and arbitrary. But these laid the
foundation for the new system of feudal taxation, which ran
up and down the social scale, with payments imposed by the
king upon his nobles (when he exercised true authority
over them, which was not very often); by the nobles upon
their lesser vassals; by these in turn upon the plebeians and
peasants. By the time of the Norman Conquest of England,
a fairly organic system had been established on the Conti-
nent, particularly in France, and this was brought to England and endures in part to this day.

The general Old French term for tax was *taille,* from
Vulgar Latin *taliare,* "to cut" (we still speak of "taking a
cut"). The *taille* could be *royale* (imposed by the king),
seigneuriale (imposed by or upon the *seigneur,* or local
overlord), *servile* (imposed upon the commoners or serfs).
These were ordinary taxes. There was also an extraordinary, occasional tax that went by the Latin name of *aux-
ilia,* the French name of *aide,* the English name of "aid."
This was paid to the baron by his vassals and underlings to
take care of a special occasion, such as the wedding of the
baron's daughter. In the case of the king, who normally was
supposed to *vivre de son domaine* ("live on the revenues of

his own estates"), it might serve to gather ransom money if the king was captured, as happened to Richard the Lion-hearted on his return from the Crusades. The form of "aid" devised on that occasion was a tax on movable property.

But the forms and names of taxes were legion: *queste* ("quest"), *tonlieu* (a form of indirect tax), *gabelle* (salt tax), *douane* (customs duty), *octroi* (local market tax, entry duty for produce coming to the city from the country), *croupe* (unofficial "tax" taken as graft by the tax collector), *mise et prise* ("put-and-take," two special forms of "aid"). The lord had the right to a *taille à volonté* ("tax at will"); but he could also be magnanimous and declare a *taille abonnée*, or canceled tax (what we might call a "forgiven tax"). In the early days of the French monarchy there were taxes that still went by Latin names: *rotaticum,* a tax on the individual wheels of vehicles; *pontaticum,* a bridge toll; *portaticum,* a portage toll; later there was a *focaticum,* or *fouage* (from *feu,* "fire"), a tax on hearths or open fireplaces, which still later became a sort of poll tax paid by the head of each family. The *carrucaticum,* or *carruage,* was a tax on plows; the *scutage,* a tax on shields, which became something you paid in lieu of performing military service. Taxes could, of course, be paid in kind, like the ancient tithes, or in forced labor (the *corvée,* where local peasants were pressed into service to build roads and bridges, or even castles). Sharecropping (*métayage*) had one interesting tax feature, which lasted until the French Revolution: all taxes on the land had to be paid by the sharecropper, while the landlord went scot-free. There was a *cadastre,* which was a combination land register and tax list, and the taxpayer was known as a *roturier,* which is said to go back to *rompre,* "to break," and could mean "the one who is always broke," though a more likely explanation is "owner of broken ground."

The *ancien régime* of France knew tax sharing in the form of *centimes additionelles* ("additional farthings"), a surtax imposed and collected by the central authority, along with its own taxes, but passed on to the local government. The feature of tax exemption, not too frequent in the classical world, now became generalized for certain categories: first of all, the king, who could not be taxed against himself; second, the nobility, save when called upon to render "aid" to the sovereign; most extensively of all, the Church, in all its ramifications. This form of ecclesiastical tax exemption was known as *francalmoigne* ("free alms"), and when we consider that at least one-fourth of all taxable property in medieval France belonged to the Church, we can see that the privilege we extend today to our religious, educational, charitable, and scientific institutions has a very broad precedent.

By way of contrast, the Moslem empires of the Middle Ages against which the Crusaders fought had a fairly simple system of taxation. There was a tithe on all war booty, and a *zakāt*, or "poor-rate," which was paid by all, equally and without progressive features. Non-Moslems living under Moslem rule were tolerated, but had to pay a special infidel poll tax known as *jizya,* and, if they were landowners, a land tax called *kharāj.*

English outgrowths of French feudal taxation largely duplicated the features of their model, but with some interesting additions. The French *taille* and *taillage* became "tallage" in Normanized England. The "tallage of groats," for instance, was a sort of personal income tax based on ability to pay. For individuals, it ran from fourpence a year for the very poor to one groat for middle incomes to as much as six marks for members of the nobility. It was also imposed on cities and counties. From about 1300 on, there

was a "butlerage" on imported wines ("butler" and "butlerage" come from French *bouteille,* "bottle"). "Benevo-
lence" was the name of a payment made by the wealthy of
England to King Edward IV. Nuisance taxes included
"hearth money," in imitation of the French *fouage,* and a
special tax on births, marriages, and burials, imposed in
1694 to finance one of the many wars with France. This ran
from a minimum of four shillings to a maximum of fifty
pounds. Charles I imposed the payment of "ship money,"
designed to finance a British navy, paid at first only by
seaports, later extended to inland areas.

Tax exemption for the Church and all its holdings had
existed since Anglo-Saxon days, when the Council of
Clovesho of 747 had decreed that the crown was powerless
to tax the ecclesiastic structure. The Norman kings had
shown some reluctance to relinquish the "aid" feature from
the Church, but by the time of Edward I, full exemption
had been restored. On the other hand, taxes with mixed
military and religious features were created by both France
and England in the late twelfth century, during the Crusades, under the title of *ad sustentationem Jerosolimitanae
terrae,* "for the support of the land of Jerusalem." A little
later came the "Saladin tithe," a war surtax that had to be
paid by all those who did not take the Cross and march off
to the Holy Land.

"Tunnage," on imported wines, "poundage," on all imported goods, are relatively modern, though their roots go
back to the Romans. Also fairly recent is the "window tax,"
imposed in 1697 and not repealed until 1851, on all open-
ings in a dwelling beyond the number of six. The justification for this tax was to make up for the financial deficien-
cies that resulted from the evil and widespread practice of
clipping coins. There was until recently a stamp duty upon
insurance, and the practice permitting only government-

stamped paper to be used for documents having any legal import persists to this day in many European countries.

Some lands tax certain luxury items, such as tobacco and alcoholic beverages; others turn them into government monopolies, as does our own State of Pennsylvania with packaged liquor. Italy and Japan still have government stores for the sale of salt and tobacco products, and it is illegal to buy or sell them privately.

The vocabulary of taxation varies from country to country, even when the countries speak the same official language. Our "internal revenue" is Britain's "inland revenue"; our "inheritance tax" is their "death duties"; and they use "rate" for local taxation, reserving "tax" for what is national in scope.

German has an orderly array of names of "popular" taxes: *Einkommensteuer,* "income tax"; *Grundsteuer,* "land tax"; *Vermögensteuer,* "property tax"; *Warenumsatzsteuer,* "purchase tax." One picturesque term applied to cars is *Steuerpferdestärke,* "taxable horse power." Then there is *Steueranschlag,* literally "tax attack," or even "tax assassination attempt," for tax assessment, along with a *Steuerabzug,* "tax departure," "retreat from taxes," for "tax deduction." The tax return you file with the German equivalent of Internal Revenue is *Steuererklärung,* or "tax clarification."

Another Germanic language, Dutch, uses as its term for tax *belasting,* whose root is *last,* "burden" or "load." *Belastingontduiking* is tax-dodging, or even more literally, "tax-ducking." The Swedish word for tax, *skatt,* is reminiscent of the old Anglo-Saxon unit of currency, the *sceatta,* later replaced by the shilling (the word survives in modern German *Schatz,* "treasure").

The Russian mind is literal. The word for tax is *nalog,*

"that which is laid upon you." The income tax, which the Soviets don't really believe in, since they don't believe in independent incomes, is *podokhodnyi nalog* (the root of the word for income, *dokhod,* means "a coming into").

Among the Romance languages, two general tendencies are noticeable. One is to make the taxpayer feel good by calling him a "contributor" (French *contribuable,* Spanish *contribuyente,* Italian *contribuente*). Both French and Spanish use "contribution" as their favorite word for tax, although the equivalents of "impost" and "tax" are also used. The other is the tendency to "perceive" or "exact" taxes rather than "collect" them. The French tax agent is a *percepteur,* the Spanish *exactor,* the Italian *esattore.* The Spanish term comes from the same root as *El Exigente,* "the demanding one," made famous by TV coffee advertising. Portuguese has a picturesque term for imposing taxes, *lançar impostos,* to "launch" or "hurl" taxes at the victim. The Spanish *censo* is not merely "census," but also "tax list." Spanish still uses the old "gabelle" (*gabela*) for an excise tax, while Italian has a term out of the Florentine Middle Ages, *balzello* (the root is *balzare,* "to jump"), for a tax imposed once in a while, like our "temporary" taxes that become permanent. What we call an "inheritance tax" and the British a "death duty" is known to the Italians as a *tassa di successione,* "succession tax." An import duty is *tassa di consumo,* "consumption tax," and the customs inspection bears the euphemistic title of *visita della dogana,* "customs visit." Tea is never served in the course of the "visit."

Enough has been said to prove beyond a doubt: (a) the universality of taxation across time and space; (b) the infinite variety of terms and euphemisms by which the various phases of the institution are known. There is another American saying that applies to taxes even more than it does to its ostensible subject matter, and we hereby paraphrase it: "Everybody talks about taxes, but nobody ever does anything about them."

11

The Voice of the Pentagon— Grunts from the Grunts

The tongue of the higher military echelons has in the past been equated with ordinary bureaucratic Gobbledegook, and there is little doubt that the same mental processes are at work in both. But Pentagonese is in addition marked by a characteristic element of understatement, the opposite of the bombastic exaggeration of Madison Avenue. This is due to the fact that its ultimate merchandise is death, which is unpleasant to most of us. Death must be sugar coated to make it acceptable, and "acceptable" is precisely one of the terms that illustrate the military language in its upper reaches: "acceptable damage," "acceptable losses," "acceptable casualties"—what a nation can take without actually going under.

The military language sometimes trickles down from the Commander-in-Chief himself. President Nixon seems responsible for the modest "sufficiency" that has replaced our earlier vaunted "superiority" in atomic and missile fields, as well as in land and naval strength. The term, which goes back to 1495, is defined as adequacy, enough for the purpose on hand; it might be paraphrased with a coined "enoughness." We hope it will be just that, though we will admit that the former "superiority" was more reassuring. "One-upmanship," which has to do with superiority, is defined in Webster Third as the art of going your competitor one better, and the illustrative sample is from the writings of Edmund Wilson. The term "one up" was apparently first used in golf in 1910, and means that you have one stroke advantage over your opponent.

More recently we have had the controversy over the defense of cities (or missile sites) by means of an "ABM" (antiballistic missile), all of which is linked with what the military call "first-strike capability" (this means that your first atomic missile blow is so devastatingly effective as to knock out your opponent's retaliatory capacity; it differs from the older "pre-emptive strike," which was designed to knock out a prospective future opponent while he still lacked his defense or retaliation capacity).

Many of the innovations of the military stem from the Vietnam war. Here we find not only those reprehensible and often deplored terms, "kill ratio" and "body count" (they have been in use for some years, yet none of our dictionaries records them), but also "greenbacking," used to describe the hiring of mercenary troops, or the financing of such responsive governments as those of South Vietnam and Cambodia, which is likewise unreported in any dictionary ("greenback" itself, for U.S. currency, goes back to 1778; perhaps there is a semantic link with the earlier [1947] "bankrolling," used in theatrical circles to signify an "angel's" financing of a show). "To headquarter" (as in "the general was headquartered in the castle") is current in military usage, though its use as a verb was found unacceptable to 90 percent of American Heritage's panel of consultants.

Curious military euphemisms are occasionally coined by the press, as when the *Los Angeles Times* reported that some G.I.'s were killed by a "friendly grenade," which proved to be just as deadly as if it had been "hostile."

Then there is the jocular yet somewhat grim game of "Chicken of the Sea," coined by our airmen in their confrontations in the Mediterranean with Soviet fliers who buzz our warships and vice-versa. The object of the game is to "escort" the other aircraft by flying parallel and very close to it. Whichever of the two fliers breaks the formation first is labeled "Chicken of the Sea."

"Protective reaction" is Pentagonese for operations like Cambodia and Laos, and displays the euphemistic quality of the language of the generals. There is "accidental delivery of ordnance equipment," meaning that we have bombed or shelled our own troops or those of our allies by mistake. "Protective encirclement" means to send in troops to rescue grounded copter pilots. "Mobile maneuvering," used for a planned withdrawal which does not always go quite according to plan, is reminiscent of the "options," "alternatives," and "contingency plans" of the Kennedy and Johnson administrations with which the Ellsberg–*New York Times* documents have made us familiar, while the "Free Fire Zones" abundantly described in connection with My Lai and other incidents remind us that during World War II entire cities with all their inhabitants were treated in exactly similar fashion by our bombing planes, though the term had not yet been devised. But then, World War II was a holy crusade in a noble cause, and everything was justified.

On occasion the Pentagon borrows expressions from other fields. The Laos campaign was described in some military quarters as "counter-productive," a term usually reserved for the field of medicine.

Civilian aviation is responsible for the statement that a particular airplane crash was caused by the pilot's "failure to maintain sufficient altitude to avoid neighboring terrain," but it was the air force that coined an expression to replace "demonstration," previously used for an accounting review of a contract, to which General Taylor had objected on the ground that "demonstration" had become a dirty word in other connections. He suggested "audit review" as a replacement, but the staff writers gave him more than he had bargained for: "Data Accounting Flow Assessment," with a suitable abbreviation, "DAFA."

"Feaseless" for unfeasible, and "disestablish" for to close down an installation are attributed to the army. "Vietnamization" and "winding down the war" seem to stem from the President's staff writers. They are balanced by a journalistic "expectation gap" and the use of "moratorium" by antiwar demonstrators. The dictionaries define the word as a deferment or delay of any action, not its actual cessation; but its use is justified by a desire to declare a "moratorium" on "business as usual" while the war is still in progress.

A curious document issued by the U.S. Command in Vietnam has to do with a guidance directive banning the use of certain terms (unofficially styled "nonos") and replacing them with other, approved terms. Appropriately, the directive is titled "Let's Say It Right!"

To a philologist, this is reminiscent of the *Appendix Probi*, a third-century A.D. listing of what people should and should not say if they wished to speak "correct" Latin rather than the awful jargon that was already beginning to degenerate into the later Romance languages. It is true that, unlike the *Appendix Probi,* "Let's Say It Right!" has a decided political slant. Nevertheless, there are enough popular terms given to afford us clear indication of the language of the privates as distinguished from that of the Pentagon. Following the styling of the *Appendix Probi,* which listed the proper word, then followed it with "not," then gave the condemned term (*"oculus, non oclus"; oculus* is the correct Latin word for eye; but *oclus,* the slang form, is what eventually goes on to become Italian *occhio,* Spanish *ojo,* French *oeil*), we shall list the Pentagonistically correct expressions first and then the enlisted men's forms, preceded by "not":

> "civilian irregular defense soldier," not "mercenary"
>
> "search and clear," not "search and destroy" (sounds less bloodthirsty, no?)
>
> "Military Assistance Command daily press briefings," not "5 o'clock follies"
>
> "regional forces," not "ruff-puff"
>
> "Vietcong," not "National Liberation Front"
>
> "Vietcong extortionists," not "Vietcong tax collectors"
>
> "rallier" or "returnee," not "(Vietcong) deserter or defector"
>
> "enemy killed," not "body count"
>
> "develop community spirit," not "hearts and minds of the people"
>
> "redeployment or replacement," not "U.S. troop withdrawal or pullout"
>
> "light and scattered action," not "lull"

From this scattered sampling, one thing is clear: the Pentagon either has changed its mind about some of its own terminology, or was not responsible for it in the first place. Some of the condemned terms are obviously jocular soldier talk; others could easily be of journalistic origin. One journalist, John Roche, had already voiced a protest against the use of the word "mercenaries" to describe what would be called "volunteers" if they were on the other side. "Mercenaries," he justly claims, has overtones of the Hessians hired by George III to put down the American Revolution. In the same vein, he speaks of "seeking a 'political' rather than a 'military' solution."

The "doughboy" of World War I and the "G.I. Joe" of World War II have turned into "grunts," so far as the Vietnam war is concerned. While "grunt," both as a noun and as a verb, goes back to the sixteenth century, only Webster Third among our dictionaries gives the acceptance of the noun as a ground lineman employed by public utilities as a helper to the man who is up on a ladder doing the actual repairs. It volunteers the suggestion that he may have been called a "grunt" because of the noises he made as he lifted and passed on heavy objects. Wentworth and Flexner offer a further connection with the suggestion that the army "grunt" was in origin a member of the Signal Corps. If all this is true, the question is, How did the Signal Corps usage become extended to cover all armed forces members? However this may be, recent innovations in usage are few and down-to-earth. The picturesque, unprintable vocabulary of the enlisted man was developed, for the most part, during the two world wars.

It is altogether uncertain whether an expression like "to freak out," which appears in none of our major dictionaries, even of slang, originated in Vietnam or in the Youth Movement. The noun "freak," in the sense of whim or prank, first appears in 1563; the sense of monstrosity, as in "freak show," is added in 1847; the sense of homosexual, in the early twentieth century. The only dictionary use of "freak" as a verb is in the sense of to speckle or streak something with color.

There is a use of "to waste" in the sense of to kill, not offered in even our most recent dictionaries, but heard repeatedly in connection with the My Lai testimony and elsewhere. "To lay waste" goes back to Middle English, and there is an antiquated legal use of "to waste" in the sense of to destroy property (but not human life). From 1689 on we find "to waste" (to do away with) used in connection with such impersonal things as sin and sorrow. Shakespeare comes a shade closer to modern usage in "Would he were wasted, marrow, bones and all!" Wentworth and Flexner claim that the verbal use of "to waste" originated with teen-age gangs, becoming current in the 1950s in the sense of to defeat decisively, to destroy. This is still not the precise counterpart of "We were ordered to waste all the villagers," and it is possible that the ultimate semantic shift took place in Vietnam.

National Observer informs us in an editorial that the cry "Kill! Kill!" formerly used in bayonet practice, is now considered an "indiscreet slogan" by the new training manuals, and is currently replaced by "Yah! Yah!" which is in better taste, though the bayonet thrust is presumably just as deadly.

Still in popular use, apparently, is the callous "turkey shoot" to describe shooting from a helicopter at fleeing Vietnamese (North and Cong only, we hope). It, too, would seem to tend to "brutalize" recruits, and might have been mentioned in "Let's Say It Right!" issued by the U.S. Command in Vietnam, which I referred to earlier in this chapter.

Other creations of the grunt mind are "Yanigan" for a crazy soldier who shoots anything in sight (this seems to have been coined by Private Charles A. West in connection with the Song My [or Pinksville] massacre of March 16, 1968). "Fragging" is the murder of officers and noncoms by rolling fragmentation grenades into their quarters, a practice that is very often drug induced. One expression, used by President Nixon in 1971 and attributed by him to General Creighton Abrams, is "hack," as in "Hack it—the Vietnamese can!" Safire views it as a variant of "cut it" or "cut the mustard."

One usage that can in no way be described as a recent innovation, and is in widespread, almost universal use wherever there are radio or other long-distance communications within or among the services, is the verb "read" in "Do you read me?" "I read you loud and clear." Oxford and Random House do not report this meaning for "read"; Webster Third and American Heritage do. Wentworth and Flexner give it as arising in air force use during World War II, and becoming current by 1950, with its equivalent "to dig" (but "read" is more intellectual, they add).

Without going into extensive research, I have the impression that this use of "read" antedates World War II. Medieval works often speak of "reading" the emblazoned devices on armor and military tunics. Knights who were illiterate could nevertheless "read" heraldic devices, in the same fashion that our later illiterates could "read" the barber's pole, the pawnbroker's three balls, and the cigar-store wooden Indian. The semantic equivalence of the roots meaning "see," "hear," "know," and "understand" goes all the way back to Indo-European (Latin and Slavic *vid-*, "to see"; Greek *void-*, "to hear"; Anglo-Saxon *wit, wot*, "to know"; Sanskrit *Veda*, "knowledge," "understanding").

The expression that meets most favor in the eyes of the grunts is without doubt "derosing," an anagram somewhat imperfectly formed from "date of estimated return from overseas." It is equivalent to "heading back to the world."

Right, Left, and Center

The language of politics is constantly being enriched from all sides. Now and then, among the coinages, there comes to light a half-forgotten term that is legitimized by the dictionaries, such as "psephology," the study of elections. This comes from the customary Greek *logos* combined with *psephos,* "pebble," and its justification is that in ancient times elections in Athens were determined by the counting of pebbles, a primitive form of ballot. Again, there are imaginative formations by the newscasters, such as "to press the flesh," meaning that the candidate goes out handshaking among his prospective constituents. (Is baby-kissing included in the term?)

These are neutral, nonpartisan terms. Equally neutral, since it is supported by all parties (though not by identical methods), is the recently proposed "tax-sharing," which in its original concept means that since the federal government bleeds the taxpayers dry and leaves little or nothing for the state and local governments to fasten their teeth into, it should turn back some of its loot to those state and local governments to use as they see fit, and not as the federal government dictates. But this simple formula arouses serious opposition.

One term that has gained new acceptance is "Middle America." This is defined in all dictionaries as a geographical unit embracing Central America, Mexico, and often the islands of the Caribbean. The term, not too often used in English, which prefers a separate listing of the component parts, is much favored in German (*"Nord-Amerika, Süd-Amerika, und Mittel-Amerika"*). There is another geographical use of "Middle" in connection with states (the "Middle States" are defined in some dictionaries, mostly British, as being those intermediate between New England and the South: New York, New Jersey, Pennsylvania, Delaware, sometimes Maryland). Casual questioning brings out the fact that most of the uninitiated, when they hear "Middle America," think of the Central or Midwestern States. The new political acceptance, however, is social-economic rather than geographic, pointing to the middle classes or middle-income groups, which constitute at least 60 percent of our population (as against the 30 percent poor and the 10 percent rich). The implications are that "Middle America" tends to vote as a unit in defense of its class interests, which does not seem too well borne out by the facts. One additional use of the term among the younger generations is that part of America which is middle-aged, established, and impervious to change.

"Silent majority" has been with us for a while, but comes up perennially every time there is an election or a demonstration, in spite of which it is ignored by the dictionaries. Again, the implication is that there exists a group, constituting a majority of the voters, which normally does not demonstrate or even raise its voice, but reveals its true feelings at the polls. To the extent that this may be true (the indications are mixed), the question arises, Why is this majority silent? Is it far too busy working to provide sustenance not only for itself, but also for those who are engaged in noisy demonstrations? It was pointed out in this connection that the "Hard Hats" held their Wall Street demonstration during their lunch hour, unlike the students who were perennially "on strike" from their classes.

Impatience with the linguistic creations of the student demonstrators is indicated by ironical inventions offered by writers who cannot be classed as right wing. Starting with "racism," which is long established, Russell Baker in his *New York Times* column goes on to present the "politicization" and "radicalization" of the campus, which have appeared elsewhere, then proceeds to "conservativization," "reactionarification," and "antinegritudinarianism," which have not, save at his hands. "Deactivated activists" and "demilitarized militarists" are offered in a spirit of irony by others, along with the "Custeristic Weathermen" (just what does "Custeristic" mean in this connection?) and the "consumerism activists," said of people like Ralph Nader who cater to the interests of consumers no matter what industrial or commercial toes they may happen to tread on. (Nader's own description of the army of lawyers, ecologists, economists, accountants, and engineers who have rallied to his banner is "public interest lawyers," etc., or "consumers' servicemen.")

Some choice creations of the political right are "Hanoi Hawks," applied by Roche to the SDS and other supporters of North Vietnam, and "unpersons," which the same writer uses as a label for Communist leaders who have fallen from grace, like Poland's Gomulka and the late Nikita Khrushchev. There is also Alsop's sarcastic description of a "Liberal Establishment" where the liberals speak only to the liberals, and Galbraith speaks only to God. "Liblash" was coined by Lenore Romney in the course of her unsuccessful Michigan senatorial campaign; she stated that a "liblash" exerted by the women's liberation movement had hurt her chances. Then there is "retroactive self-righteousness," coined by Ben Wattenberg to describe the attitude of senators who voted full powers to Johnson for the Vietnam war, but later stridently regretted the decisions he had made in accordance with their mandate. "Skull-duggery rooms" is columnist Cuneo's description of the caucus rooms at the Democratic convention.

By far the most colorful right-wing contributions to language were made in the course of the 1970 campaign by Vice-President Agnew. Whether the catchwords, slogans, and clichés that poured from his lips were his own creations or those of his White House aide William Safire is still undetermined. Starting out with forms like "troglodytic" and "effete snobs," he went on to alliterative gems worthy of the poetic genius of the Anglo-Saxons: "pusillanimous pussy-footing," "politicians of panic," "purveyors of pessimism," "troubadours of trouble," "vicars of vacillation"; then, warming up to the literary device, "nattering nabobs of negativism," "covey of confused congressmen," "hopeless, hysterical hypochondriacs of history," "fumbling flugelman of Fun City." His political opponents tried to reply in kind by dubbing him a "functional alliterate" and denouncing his "lurid lexicon of 'literation" (candidate Muskie even came out with "an Agnewesque game of golf"); but they were hopelessly outgunned. La Guardia's denunciation of "punks, tinhorns and gamblers," back in the 1930s, was only a faint foretaste of the Agnevian language, and President Nixon's "apostles of defeatism and doubt," voiced at an address to a Knights of Columbus convention, may be described as a faint after-echo.

But the political left does not down easily. James Reston, in the columns of *The New York Times,* described the new Washington cult of "Agnewsticism" as a doctrine that the truth is safer in the hands of politicians than in those of the news media, and that the administration is always right, especially when it's wrong.

Other phases of the right-wing movement were mercilessly criticized and satirized. The late Drew Pearson painted the Young Americans for Freedom as "an extreme right-wing group with ties to the John Birch Society." Nixon's "making things perfectly clear" and his "Southern Strategy" came in for their innings. What had originally been called "Nixonomics" was later described as "Nixon's Economic Game Plan," though a nation's economy does not seem a suitable subject for games. Still later, when the 1971 price-wage freeze went into effect, it was criticized by the AFL–CIO leaders as being too favorable to capital at the expense of labor, and the ironical "trickle-down theory" was coined to describe Mr. Nixon's views on how to restore the economy. It is only fair to add that "Nixonomics" was more recently paralleled by "McGovernomics," coined by the financial editor of *The New York Times,* and columnist Peter Lisagor, on May 16, 1972, presented us with "Lyndonology," "Nixonology," and "Nixon watchers."

Nixon's German or German-American advisers (Kissinger, Haldeman, Klein, Kleindienst, Ziegler, Schultz) have been dubbed collectively the "German Mafia" (Kennedy's "Irish Mafia" will be remembered). Other names for them are "the Fourth Reich," "the Berlin Wall," and "All the King's Krauts."

NEP, or "New Economic Policy," was reinterpreted by candidate Humphrey into "Nixon's Economic Propaganda," while columnist Mary McGrory devised "Son of Freeze" for Nixon's Phase Two.

Columnist Jack Anderson, in his column for December 30, 1971, used a construction which may have been accidental, but may also be highly misleading to the reader. Criticizing Nixon's policy with regard to the India-Pakistan conflict, Anderson says: "Thereby he [obviously Nixon] aligned the United States against the Bengalis, whose freedom Yahya had brutally repressed. He [who? Yahya or Nixon?] overturned their free election, jailed their elected leader and sent troops to terrorize the populace."

"Creeping inflation," a right-wing creation, was expanded into "creeping recovery" by the left. "Lawnorder" was compressed to betoken the semiliteracy of its believers. The wealthier classes were sarcastically described as "pillars of the community," and Philip Barry remarked that "there is no prettier picture than the privileged class enjoying its privileges." Coined terms included John Roche's "midlash" to describe the use of the full middle name of Hubert Horatio Humphrey by Goldwater to cast a slur and win the votes of people who reduce middle names to initials. "The Sage of Johnson City" was used by Mary McGrory to describe a certain former President. "The Hippies as Contrameritocracy" was the title of an article in *Intellectual Digest,* and "Amerika" was so spelled by the New Left to indicate that the country was going over to a Nazi-type dictatorship (unfortunately, they forgot that *Amerika* happens to be the Russian as well as the German way to spell our country's name).

The political slogan was the subject of an interesting article by right-winger William Safire in *The New York*

Times Magazine for December 26, 1971. Starting back in the middle of the nineteenth century ("We Polk'd you in 1844, we shall Pierce you in 1852"), he goes on to the Great Depression ("In Hoover we trusted, now we are busted"), then to the Johnson-Goldwater struggle of 1964 ("In your guts you know he's nuts!"), then comes down to our own day and the welter of candidates of 1972 ("Ready for Teddy?"; "Trust Muskie," with its variant "Trusk Musty"; "Ch - rist! What charisma!"; "Cities are not unmcgovernable"; "Clean McGovernment"; "Govern for McPresident!"; "Welcome Abroad!" presumably meant for Lindsay and Yorty; "Nixon's through in '72" and "Nixon sticks till '76"; and an all-purpose "Throw the rascals in!" He might have added "Four more years!"). He reaches the ultimate conclusion: "Slogans are not enough!"

Safire is a rightist who does not hesitate to satirize his own side. Neither do some leftists. McGovern, for instance, labeled Muskie "high in the straddle," while someone else devised "Clean Gene" for McCarthy.

More serious, if less humorous, slogans are the new-fangled "Power to the People!" (What people? Those demonstrating?) and "Hell, no! We won't go!" to signify resistance to the draft. The use of "community" in the place of the older "neighborhood," and the title of a book such as *The Greening of America* may also have political significance. The verbal use of "green" is limited to the meaning of to make or become green; but Oxford reports a slang use arising in 1884, "to hoax." "Community" has long been established; but at an earlier period it usually meant either a separate entity, like a suburban area, or the country at large ("the American community"). In places like New York City people generally spoke of what went on in their neighborhood, not in their community, which in this context seems to have political, not to say leftist, overtones.

"Community," however, should not be confused with "commune," which columnist Roche describes as the modern version of the old "co-op." "Commune" is an ancient word that goes back to Vulgar Latin and Medieval French. In modern French, it is a small territorial division governed by a mayor and a municipal council. The two Paris Communes of 1792 and 1871 were revolutionary bodies which functioned during the Terror and the siege of Paris; both were eventually overthrown by the forces of reaction. In modern hippie parlance, a "commune" is a community unofficially established for group living, with all that such living entails.

Two other terms have recently undergone subtle change of meaning: "ethnic" and "priorities." Take, for example, the meaning that attaches to "ethnic" in a statement made by Barbara Mikulski of the Southeast Community Organization of Baltimore: "The ethnic American is sick of being stereotyped as a racist and dullard by phony white liberals, pseudo black militants, and patronizing bureaucrats."

"Ethnic," the dictionaries inform us, first came into the language in 1470 with a Biblical meaning: pertaining to nations not Christian or Jewish; Gentile, heathen, pagan. "Ethnos," however, has in Greek the pre-Biblical meaning of nation or group, without specification of cleavage into more- or less-favored groups. Around the middle of the nineteenth century, ethnology became the science dealing with races and peoples, again without specific reference. There is general agreement among the dictionaries that "ethnic" should mean pertaining to a religious, racial, national, or cultural group. Random House adds the factor of language; Webster Third that of physical and mental traits and common heritage. All equate "ethnic" with "racial," and Webster Third goes so far as to exemplify its racial, linguistic, and cultural groups with a parenthesis that runs: "(Negroes, Irish, Italians, Germans, etc.)."

But in recent times there has grown the tendency to make "racial" refer to such nonwhite groups as blacks, American Indians, occasionally (and erroneously) Mexican-Americans and Puerto Ricans, while reserving "ethnic" for white groups that had their origins in Europe (Italians, Germans, Irish, Slavs, Greeks, etc.). This usage opposes "racial" groups to "ethnic" groups, and seems designed to deepen cleavages that unfortunately exist among groups of American citizens of different "racial" or "ethnic" origins. In the final analysis, it tends to set off white groups that are not of Anglo-Saxon extraction from those whose color runs from black to light brown. Along with "minority groups" and other similar terms, this usage tends to disrupt our national unity, and is to that extent weasely.

Concerning "priorities," there is no difference in the basic meanings. (Legally, priorities means precedence among claims or order of payment; otherwise, precedence by order of importance or urgency, sometimes in the matter of obtaining supplies in times of shortage, or in the matter of attention in connection with competing alternatives). The term "priorities," however, is getting to be increasingly used by groups concerned with the betterment of certain classes of our population, usually to the detriment of the requirements of sound military defense or of such supposed frills as the space program. "Cut down military appropriations and moon explorations, and use the money on the big-city ghettoes" seems to be the slogan. Without going too deeply into the merit of expenditures to improve the lot of the poor, it may be remarked that in a world where international relations are still subject to the ultimate arbitration of military force, it may be highly unwise to weaken ourselves to the point where a foreign power with an ideology that differs radically from our own could conceivably be in a position to dictate not only our foreign, but even our internal, policies. The record of such powers in improving the lot of their own less-fortunate classes is not such as to inspire emulation.

The language of the Extreme Left in recent times is perhaps best brought out by Arnold Beichman in "Six Big Lies about the American Underground Press." To begin with, "underground" is the wrong term for organs that are sold openly on the newsstands; but this is illustrative of weasel word inaccuracy. Terms appearing in the "underground" press that further reveal the nature of the Extreme Left Wing and its leanings are the distinction made between "incipient [or preventive] Fascism," the sort of thing that is alleged to exist even now in "Amerika," and "real" Fascism, Hitler or Mussolini style, that is supposed to be the ultimate outcome of the former; the use of "creative disorder" for vandalism; terms like "cultural, ethnic, psychic genocide," again said to prevail in our society, and even "Bomber Left," a term in which the extremists glory. Rennie Davis, in an address to his erstwhile Mayday followers, labeled the U.S. government a "racist, sexist government."

Of interest also are items that come from abroad and give some insight into the nature and practices of Communism. From Italy, for example, it is pointed out that "comrade" (*camerata*) is now the term used among themselves by the Neo-Fascists, while the Communists have gone back to the old Socialist usage of "companion" (*compagno*). The Chinese Communist press continues, despite the Ping-Pong Era, to describe the governments of South Korea, South Vietnam, Taiwan, and other such nations as the "running dogs" of American capitalistic imperialism. But the Chinese Communists also charge the Soviets with

"Social Imperialism" (to which the Soviet reply is "Social Traitors!"), and describe the efforts of the United States and Russia at disarmament as "a duet of negativism."

An Italian periodical, *Il Sedicesimo,* publishes parts of a "Glossary of Chinese Communist Terms." Once the difficulties of translation into a Western language are overcome, the "Glossary" is a revealing index of the Communist mind in full operation. One feature that strikes me in the extended sampling at my disposal is the impressive use of numbers ("The Fighters of the Five Virtues"; "The Three-in-One Combination"; "The Five Requisites"; "The Sixteen-Point Decision"; "The Ten Points of the Central Committee"; "The Twenty-three-article Document"; "The Three-Family Village"; "The Eight Points for Attention"; "The Four Priorities"; "The Four Clean-ups"; "The Four Old Relics"; "The Three-Eight Working Style"; "The Three Rules for Discipline"). Is this a feature of a narrow, mathematical, pseudoscientific way of thought? Or is it something that stems from the depths of the Far Eastern mind? It may be remarked that there is a parallel in South Vietnam President Thieu's "Four-No Policy" ("No Coalition; No Neutralism; No Communist Party; No Land Concessions to the Communists").

Proceeding more in depth into the singular Chinese document, we find that the "Five Virtues for Fighting Men" are described as "excelling in political and ideological work," "in military techniques," "in fulfilling fighting assignments," "in keeping fit," and "in three-eight labor" (so called because in Chinese it is expressed by three phrases and eight characters; the former are "firm and correct political orientation," "simple and efficient style," and "flexibility in tactics and strategy"; the eight written characters boil down to four concepts: unity, vigilance, honesty, liveliness).

The five requisites or virtues mandatory for good revolu-

tionists are to be pure Marxist-Leninists; to serve the cause
of the Chinese masses and those of the entire world; to be
able to bind and work with the majority; to serve as examples of democratic centralism within the Party; to be
neither arrogant nor hasty, but imbued with the spirit of self-
criticism.

Among the Ten-Point Decisions are the following: to
overthrow those leaders who take the capitalistic road; to
repudiate the authority of bourgeois reactionaries and the
ideology of the exploiting classes; to transform education,
literature, and art to conform to the new Socialist economic
structure.

The Eight Points for the Attention of Popular Liberation
Armies are to discuss politely; to pay for what you buy; to
return what you borrow; to indemnify for what you damage; not to strike or offend people; to respect crops; not to
take liberties with women; not to mistreat prisoners. The
Four Priorities: between man and weapons, choose man;
between political and other work, choose the political; between routine and ideology, choose the latter; between
ideas in books and ideas circulating among the living
masses, again choose the latter. The Four Things to Be
Cleaned Up are politics, ideology, organization, and the
economy. The Four Items to Be Gotten Rid Of: bourgeois
ideology, culture, morality, and habits. The Three Rules for
Discipline: obey orders at all times; don't take a pin or a
thread from the masses; hand in everything you confiscate.
The Ultimate Principle, "Unity-Criticism-Unity," means
that starting from a feeling of unity you solve contradic-
tions through self-criticism and struggle, thus achieving a
new unity on a new basis.

In our future relations with the People's Republic of
China, this is the mentality with which we will have to cope.
There is no doubt that it has praiseworthy features, at least

in theory, particularly for what regards personal honesty and the spirit of self-sacrifice on behalf of the community. It also has an element of blind fanaticism that brooks no opposing views, and is completely at loggerheads with our own principles of individual freedom and nonviolent dissent. Is coexistence possible with a nation headed by a leader who once bitterly remarked that "the moon in America is rounder than the moon in China"? But then the Chinese Communists' own description of the forthcoming "Dance of the Bear and the Dragon" may permit the Eagle to continue to soar above both.

13

Is There a Black Language?

On the racial front, we have the now almost universal shift from Negro to black. A few linguistically conservative media continue the use of "Negro," defying the frowns of the leaders of the Black Establishment. "Nonwhite" was suggested as a replacement. But in addition to being inexact (after all, there are plenty of nonwhites besides blacks), it is also a poor euphemism. This was ably pointed out by Dr. Nathan Wright, who calls "nonwhite" inherently exclusive, and claims that it has the effect of setting black men apart as being nonpersons, and certainly non-Americans. "The aggressive affirmation of blackness," he goes on, "is a beneficent reminder to us all that no man can be 'just like' or even 'equal to' another."

There is also James Forman's "reparations," demanded, in financial form, of the churches and synagogues to repay the blacks for both past slavery and continuing discrimination. One might wonder why churches and synagogues were made the targets of the demand rather than worthier institutions (local governments, business concerns, and real estate interests come to mind). The point of view involved is perhaps explained in a letter written to *The New York Times* by a white man in Michigan, which is also, in its final reaches, a gem of demonstration of the "new" language of our times. It reads in part: "We WASPS and other whites . . . have been asked, if not compelled, to come out of our churches and comfortable pews in order to *confront the issues* the outside world is raising. The church must be *relevant* and '*within the world*,' and many more of us will have to get much more *meaningfully involved* in a *committed* and *purposeful* way [my italics]."

All this, however, does not add up to a language. But there is a recent work by Hermese Roberts entitled *The Third Ear: A Black Glossary* ("third ear," by the way, is an expression taken from African storytellers, who ask their audiences to "lend a third ear" when they want more attention). This offers such choice bits as "Man, he's putting down his Ralph Bunche to his old lady" (he's talking his way out of a tight situation by the use of diplomatic language), and "the day the eagle flies," meaning payday. Other coinages reported are "landprop" (a telescoping of "landlord" and "proprietor"), "rap" for talk and "hang-up" for preoccupation (but the last two have been around for a while, and have penetrated the general teen-age language), "rip off" for steal, "squeeze" for a girl- or boy-friend, "sweatbox" for a crowded party, "happy shop" for liquor store. There is also a curious inversion of "bad" to mean good, or stylish. Hermese Roberts' *Glossary* has been distributed in pamphlet form by the English Language Institute of America to over 2,000 organizations and bodies that employ large numbers of black workers.

There is a more serious side to "Black English," represented by the current controversy over the desirability of teaching black children in their "native" tongue rather than forcing them into the difficult situation of using ordinary English. The division on this issue does not at all follow the color line. Many white linguists, and even some foundations that have furnished grants for the purpose, believe in teaching "Black English," which is a course supported by some black extremist leaders. But just as many black leaders and white educators have pointed out not only that "Black English" is also spoken by poor southern whites, but that confirming black children in the use of what amounts to a dialect serves on the one hand to perpetuate segregation and separatism and on the other hand to retard young blacks in the ascent to full equality to which they are entitled. Nonmanual occupations normally require the use of standard English. *The Crisis,* one of the organs of the NAACP, states forcefully: "Black parents throughout this nation should rise up in unanimous condemnation of this insidious conspiracy to cripple their children permanently."

In connection with the educational process, the term "quality education" has come to be regarded by some as a weasely expression designed to circumvent school integration through the bussing of pupils. In theory, "quality education" should be extended to all, in poorer as well as in more affluent school districts, and all politicians are strongly in favor of it. The question is how to achieve it in practice instead of paying it lip service while doing nothing, or next to nothing. The compulsory bussing offered as a fast-working alternative, however, presents its own thorny problems.

Roberts notes that blacks have more terms for whites than whites have for blacks, which may or may not be true. There is one highly resented white word used in addressing a black, "boy," which had a strange, "nonblack" outcropping during the great Student Rebellion. President Pusey of Harvard was televised as he rapped with some student leaders, none of whom was black. Mild and inoffensive as he was, the elderly Prexy nevertheless at one point addressed one of the students as "boy." The recipient bridled. "Boy?" he asked menacingly, lifting his eyebrows. Pusey was quick to explain that he was using the term affectionately, as a father might use it to a son. The audience was left to wonder whether the objection was merely to a term indicating an age difference, or whether it had deeper, hidden roots in a spilled-over black resentment against "boy" as a term of address.

When Roberts' *Black Glossary* first appeared, columnist Russell Baker of *The New York Times* thought it was time to issue a counterpart "White Glossary" that would interpret the language of the suburbs to the blacks. He, too, offers "Ralph Bunche," but in the sense of one of the few persons of any race who could move in next door without lowering real estate values. Baker even translates suburban "Er-uh-er" into "Like man, I mean," "Like man, y'know"; a general signal that the brain is temporarily idling.

"Pig," which to many blacks is synonymous with "policeman," is presented to them by Baker as having the secondary meaning of "a four-footed animal," often used for comparison with young sons in such expressions as "This room is not fit for a pig!" "Pig," interestingly, is a term eschewed by blacks when speaking of policemen of their own race. For them, it is either "Uncle Tom" or "handkerchief head."

But "pig" has far more extensive uses, not only in the black language but also in that of the white SDS, being extended to anyone who holds on to any shreds of traditional values. Senator Fulbright, despite his opposition to the Vietnam war, was once presented with a pig's head by

SDS members who had disguised themselves as waiters for purposes of the presentation, which Fulbright took in stride, without flinching or protesting, and with a mild display of humor.

"Pig" applied to a person as a term of opprobrium goes back to 1546 ("swine" is the older term), and Wentworth and Flexner inform us that it has been applied to policemen since 1848. Its extension to nonpolicemen who are members of the Establishment gives us pause. Could it be due to a literate memory of George Orwell's *Animal Farm,* where the pigs got to be more equal than the other animals, and consequently organized themselves into an Establishment?

But there is more. In German slang usage, "pigs" is used not for the police, but for students, with *Schweinebums* for snobs, and even a book entitled *Versuch über Schweine* ("Research About Pigs"), in the sense of students. There is also a German musical composition on "pigs," or students, by Hans Werner Henze. Language is a highly subjective sort of thing.

The coinage of "blackthink" on the analogy of "poorthink," to indicate anyone whose thinking is black-oriented, and of "Blackonomics," on the analogy perhaps of "Nixonomics," is probably of white origin. But there is also "Blacula" ("Dracula" with an all-black cast), which seems a genuine black creation. One black-originated coinage that has achieved full currency is "the real McCoy," which John Morris and Henry Sam, in their recently published *Black Calendar,* trace to Elijah McCoy, a black inventor who patented no fewer than forty-eight devices for the automatic lubrication of locomotive engines. Such extensive use was made of these inventions that heavy-duty machinery was considered incomplete if it did not have the "McCoy system." People inspecting a new piece of machinery would inquire whether it was the "real McCoy." The reassurance "It is the real McCoy" has now become a set phrase to indicate perfection.

One journalistic usage for which the blacks cannot be held responsible is the omission of any qualifying adjective in a news item if the youthful offender is black, coupled with a definite "white youth" if he is not; something that might be labeled "description by omission." A usage borrowed from the blacks is the American Indian "Uncle Tom-Tom," to describe an Indian who collaborates with the white man.

There is occasional protest against the use by black writers of terminology offensive to blacks. Eugene Gordon, writing in the *Manhattan Tribune,* deplores the use by Roy Innis of such terms as "mulattos," "house niggers," "wench, "and "runaway," which he calls "slave-breeder's terms." He concludes by accusing black militants who allow themselves to be drawn into this practice of being "mini-militants." To his list may be added the numerous terms of disparagement of the "Uncle Tom" type described in my earlier volume *Words in Sheep's Clothing.* One more such term is "Oreo," taken from the trade name of a cookie which is black on the outside, white on the inside.

It is difficult to draw precise borderlines between the vocabulary of the blacks, that of the Student Revolt, and that of the younger generations pure and simple. Consider the intrusive "like" ("It's like cold"), which even Webster Third labels substandard, and which Wentworth and Flexner describe as arising in New York City among the jazz, cool, beat classes, with a possible reinforcement from Yiddish usage, for the purpose of avoiding a too definite statement, but which has spread to the point of appearing almost universally in the speech of younger-generation members who have no intellectual pretensions, and even of some who do. If this usage arose in jazz circles, as our authors seem to think, then the heart and center of those circles is Harlem, and Harlem's inhabitants are the linguistically ingenious and creative blacks.

14

The Vocabulary of Violence

Fully organized violence is a prerogative of governments, not of groups or individuals. Its name is War, the Absolute Violence that destroys absolutely.

But there are forms of violence that can be carried on by lesser organizations, such as "mobs" or rackets. This falls under the heading "Organized Crime." The other sort of mob, engaged in violent demonstrations with resulting harm to life, limb, or property, is seldom described as downright criminal. Yet it shares with organized crime the characteristic of violence that is at least partly organized, planned, and directed. Lastly, we have the individual violence represented by "crime in the streets," also directed against life and property, but without the dubious justification supplied by a national or group ideology. Despite its relative lack of organization and direction, this is the type of violence that the average citizen fears the most, largely because of its unpredictability and its frequency of occurrence.

Governmental violence of the military variety has been described in Chapter 11. There is, however, one little-known angle represented by the grimly euphemistic term "international disposal man," a hired killer who works for a government's espionage system, and polishes off counter-spies in approved Capone style. The difference is that our international disposal men are given monetary and other rewards instead of being sent to Alcatraz. The same treatment, of course, is extended to their counterparts working for other nations. One example of their activities was the killing by members of the CIA of a Vietnamese suspected of being a double agent. The man was apparently "snatched" (an in-group word for kidnapped), interrogated, and found guilty of working for the enemy as well as for us. It was then unofficially suggested that he be "terminated with extreme prejudice" (a polite way of saying, "Rub him out!"), and the sentence was duly carried out.

The sort of violence carried on by organized crime syndicates of the Murder Incorporated type has sometimes been described as connected with the Sicilian Mafia and the native American Cosa Nostra, a term brought to the attention of a nationwide television audience by the Valachi revelations before the McClellan Committee in 1963; but these connections have just as frequently been vehemently denied. Nevertheless, they have given rise to certain semantic shifts in old, established words, shifts that have not yet gotten into our major dictionaries, even of slang, save for the very recent American Heritage: "family," in the sense not of a domestic group, but of a criminal organization; "God-father," popularized by the exceedingly popular novel and motion picture featuring Marlon Brando—a word that has not yet had time to slip even into American Heritage, but seems to be a loan-translation of Italian *compare* or *padrino,* and betokens the titular head of a "family" in the sense described above. In his recent book *From Julius Caesar to the Mafia,* Luigi Barzini offers a word, *cosca,* said to represent a grouping of "families" in the Sicilian Mafia organization. This word, which appears in none of our Italian dictionaries, may possibly be, through an accident of linguistic misunderstanding on Valachi's part, the base word of "Cosa Nostra," which apparently had never previously been heard, either in Italy or in America. "Cosca nostra," our "group of families," seems to make more sense than "Cosa Nostra," "our thing." Older terms for criminal organizations of this type are the Neapolitan *Camorra* and the American *Mano Nera,* or "Black Hand," which flourished even before prohibition and bootlegging. It was recently pointed out by another witness before a Congressional Committee that the word "Mafia" is practically never heard in the organizations that flourish in America. They prefer the native term "mob," though the term "Iron Society" is also occasionally heard.

"Vigorish," sometimes cut down to "vig" or translated as "weight," is the term used by the mobs to describe the interest on interest charged by loan sharks and their "enforcers." It is reported (with the alternative spelling "viggerish") only by Wentworth and Flexner, who claim its first appearance in 1956, and extend its meaning to the betting percentage in favor of the gambling house, or any share in the proceeds of a criminal enterprise. Wentworth and Flexner give "contract" in the sense of bribe or fix (1958), but not in the more recent meaning of "to put out a contract on someone," to hire a paid killer to dispose of a victim. To "hit" someone, the gangland counterpart of the military "to waste," is likewise absent from the *Dictionary of Slang,* though we are all familiar with it from the movies and TV. Synonyms are "to make a hit" and "to burn." "Soldiers" and "troops," as well as "enforcers," are occasionally used in referring to hired killers. It is fairly evident that some of our underworld terminology is of quite recent origin.

Another abundant source of violent vocabulary is imbedded in the language of our more questionable youth groups, particularly those that organize themselves into gangs, either for the idealistic purpose of reshaping the world or for more traditional hell-raising. One of the students' contributions, it seems, is "to trash," discussed earlier, in Chapter 4.

"Bibi" (origin unknown) for struggle, "bust" for arrest, "hassle" for harassment by police or others, are commonly used terms of the Student Revolt. The most militant branch of the SDS is the "Weatherman" faction, which takes its name from the line "You don't need a weatherman to see which way the wind blows" in Bob Dylan's "Subterranean Homesick Blues." "We don't need a weatherman, period" could well be society's response. It was also recently suggested that the big Washington demonstration by the self-styled "Mayday Tribe," which was supposed to tie up the government in knots but failed to do so, might appropriately be described as "The March of the Swine," the title of a German musical composition, *Schweinemarsch,* remembering that in German slang usage *Schwein* or "pig" refers to a student, not to a cop.

Concerning violence arising among foreign-language groups, such as the New York Puerto Ricans or the southwestern Chicanos, one suggested remedy is to arm the police with a knowledge of Spanish as well as with guns and clubs. In El Paso, Texas, such instruction includes a thorough indoctrination in Spanish swear words, along with conversations about parking tickets, accidents, crowds, parades, bars, and baby deliveries. The officers are not supposed to use the cuss words but should be able to understand them so that they will know when they are being insulted. The name "Chicano" itself, unreported in any of our dictionaries, may possibly be derived from *chico*, small (there is a term occasionally applied by the Anglos to the Spanish speakers, *hermanitos*, little brothers). Less likely seems a connection with "chicane," "chicanery," which come into English from French.

The Italian-American Unity Movement, which is neither violent nor anti-American (only anti-FBI), and sports in its demonstrations both Italian and American flags (the latter never reversed, but carried proudly at full staff), has as its slogan the unity cry "One!" Rabbi Meir Kahane's Jewish Defense League, which indulges in acts of violence against Soviet and Arab-country representatives, and has been accused of responsibility for the Hurok bombing, which it denies, has "Never again!" as its watchword.

The American "Hell's Angels," given to occasional violence, are paralleled by British youth groups who are as likely to ride bicycles as motorcycles, but are similarly committed to violence. Three such groups described by Nik Cohn, who made a study of the subject for *The New York Times,* are the "Skinheads," the "Greasers," and the "Rudys." The most numerous of the three, the Skinheads, are to some extent the heirs of the former "Mods." All their hair is shorn off their skulls, and they sport heavy boots known as "Bovverboots" ("Botherboots"), dance the "Reggae," imported from the West Indies, have "Aggro"

(Aggravation) as their byword, and delight in trouncing hippies, homosexuals, and "Pakis" (Pakistanis or East Indians). Being of lower-class origin, they hate "Swinging London" and the middle-class, long-haired hippies who prate of Love and Peace. The Rudys are Jamaicans, who know how to take care of themselves. The Pakis, on the other hand, are weak and peace-loving. The Greasers descend from the "Teddy Boys" of old, sport pony-tails and blue jeans and motor-bikes, and still worship Elvis Presley. The "Flower Power" of four years ago is gone, and scribbled on the wall of Newcastle Station in Liverpool in letters two feet high is the inscription: "Who here remembers hippies?" Such is the scene of youthful violence without a cause in a land that still prides itself on respect for law and order.

While they do not pertain to violence, there are two interesting police slang terms that were brought to the fore when Commissioner Murphy decided to investigate his own New York Finest. A few of the men were found guilty of "cooping," a term that appears in Wentworth and Flexner (1958; any shelter used by policemen to avoid the elements; from G. Y. Wells, *Station House Slang*). The precise sense is sleeping on the job, taking it easy in the patrol car instead of prowling for criminals. This dereliction was uncovered by "shoe-flies" (special detectives assigned to ferret out patrolmen in violation of rules; but this slang term is reported from as far back as 1930 by Wentworth and Flexner, with the precise meaning in which it is used today).

One curious euphemism much used by the police in describing the person accused of a crime is "perpetrator." While it may be meant to soften the odium and implications of guilt that would be conveyed by "criminal" or "offender," or even "suspect," it is only fair to point out to the

Boys in Blue that "perpetrate" bears the dictionary definition of "be guilty of, commit, perform, carry out." If it is
their idea to leave in doubt the guilt of the person they have
arrested, they are using the wrong term.

15

As Labor and Capital Clash

Organized labor is said to be acutely conscious of concepts such as "take-home pay," "portal to portal," "fringe benefits," "coffee break time," "wash-up time," "paid vacations," "paid sick time," "religious holidays," "birth leave," "funeral leave." These are terms that have been legitimized by long usage in the labor field. There are others not quite so legitimized; for instance, the "job action," which means in effect a work slowdown, such as the show staged by the New York City police not too long ago. In view of its distinctive features, it might perhaps be more accurate to call it "job inaction."

Another term that recently drew our attention is the so-called "chapel meetings," seemingly peculiar to the printing staff of *The New York Times.* This is also in the nature of a slowdown, since the meetings are called during working hours to discuss wage and other negotiations with management. Although the term appears strange in view of the customary religious meaning of "chapel," it is thoroughly sanctified by usage. Oxford gives "chapel" in the sense of an association of journeymen in a printing shop, and dates the first recorded appearance of this use in 1688. It fails to tell us how it arose. Did printers at one time meet in real chapels, out of a sense of religious devotion? Then there is what someone labeled, in connection with recent railroad strikes, the "Old Bible of Work Rules," which goes back to the nineteenth century, has never been revised, and lends itself to extensive and expensive featherbedding, the cost of which, as usual, is borne by the ultimate consumer. It may be added in this connection that it seems quite incongruous for a Congress so concerned over a 6 percent rate of general unemployment (only 2 percent above the so-called "full employment" level, which is set at 96 percent of the work force) to be so unconcerned about strikes in essential communication and transportation industries that have the effect of throwing out of work millions of workers in unrelated fields, losing billions of dollars for the economy, and causing untold discomfort to that perennial innocent bystander, John Q. Public. It is perhaps time that the unrestricted right to strike in such fields as railroads, shipping, airlines, subways and busses, telephones and telegraphs, and the mails be curtailed, in the interests of that "general welfare" of which so much of an issue is made by our liberal-minded politicians in so many other legal and political connections.

The constant use in the field of labor relations of such terms as "yellow dog" (or "sweetheart") contract, "unfair," "Boulwarism," "soulless leeches," "bloated profits," "strike deadline," has led a Los Angeles economist, Arthur H. Hawkins, to produce an interesting study on *Self-Discipline in Labor-Management Relations*, with a special chapter devoted to what he calls "The Divisive Industrial Relations Dialogue." The author holds that collective bargaining agencies should reject the hate-spawned dialogue of the nineteenth century and eliminate similar phraseology that has crept into the language in the last fifteen years. He considers management equally responsible for its use, having picked it up from early radical union leaders; government unthinkingly went along and inserted the phraseology of divisiveness and hostility into labor legislation, thus helping to foster the illusion of two armed camps in a state of perennial warfare, with only brief periods of truce.

As an illustration of his thesis, he takes the word "labor" itself. Why should the majority of U.S. citizens who work for their livelihood and that of their families be categorized as "laborers" or "toilers"? Is it to build up the illusion that they are suffering have-nots? The word "labor" historically has overtones of manual toil. Would not "paycheck population" be more truly descriptive of wage and salary earners, be they blue collar or white collar? As possible substitutes for "labor," which he calls "a demeaning, debasing word," he suggests "earning roster," "payroll," or "manpower."

He goes on to offer an entire series of replacements for words and expressions commonly used in labor relations which have fighting overtones. A sampling may prove instructive, though we have had to arrange them ourselves, since he did not place them opposite each other. With apologies for any unintentional wrong couplings, this is what we have:

Present Term	*Suggested Replacement*
boycott	cease to purchase
captive audience	involuntary audience
coercion	motivating through fear
cooling-off period	period of reconsideration

Present Term	Suggested Replacement
demand	request
discharge, fire	sever, remove
discipline	directive improvement
discrimination	evaluation
dispute	difference
disqualify	evaluate unfavorably
exploit	use without reward
fair-haired boy	favored person
featherbedding	using excess employees
grievance	problem, question
integration	merging
jurisdiction	area of operations
layoff	temporary work cessation
living wage	equitable compensation
lockout	business moratorium
masses	public
militant	active
picket	parade
prerogative	privilege
probation	provisional period
raiding	operations out of area
scab, strike-breaker	substitute, non-certified worker
segregation	distinction without evaluation
seniority	continuity
sit-down strike	work cessation on premises
slanted	purposely misdirected
slowdown	deferred schedules
steward	representative
strike, walkout, work stoppage	work cessation
sweat shop	abnormal requirement

Present Term	*Suggested Replacement*
tycoon	owner, president
tyrannical	sole authority

The writer's intention is highly praiseworthy. Would his method be effective? Would it be possible to eradicate a long-ingrained vocabulary to which everybody is accustomed and which, while it may be offensive in spots, is highly meaningful? It will be noticed that the suggested replacements are almost universally longer and more involved than the words they are meant to replace, and that a good many of them present features similar to those of bureaucratic or Pentagon gobbledegook. For some of the most offensive terms in the field ("fink," "rat," "bloated," "extortionate," "gluttonous," etc.) no replacement seems available.

The basic question is whether conflict in any field is primarily due to intemperate language or to a true clash of interests. In the field of international diplomacy, the older style, exemplified by people like Talleyrand and Metternich, called for jewels of understatement. The more modern diplomatic style, as shown by Fascist, Nazi, and Communist spokesmen, is far blunter and often openly offensive. Yet as many wars arose out of international situations in which "our government views with deepest concern the actions of a government with which we have always entertained the most friendly relations" as out of those where "we will bury the putrid democracies" or "the People's Democracies will fight to the death the inroads of the imperialistic, colonialistic capitalists."

The power of words is unquestionably great; but there is the danger that it may be overestimated. The realities of situations where national or group interests truly clash remain realities, however much one may seek to sugarcoat them. Yet it is undeniable that a more temperate use of language is desirable, if only for the sake of the language itself and of the speakers' adrenal glands.

The language of capital where it does not directly clash with labor is studded with such pleasant terms as "income," "extra dividends" (or "melons"), "growth," "appreciation," "capital gain," said to be the popular aims of the investor today. At times, purely financial terms get mixed up with government policies and give rise to gobbledegook. "Incomes policy," for instance, is based on the theory that wages, salaries, rents, and dividends are not only "incomes" to their recipients but also elements of costs that companies try to cover in their selling prices. If the incomes and costs rise no faster than the increase in productivity (or output per recipient), then price stability results, and inflationary tendencies are checked.

But this seemingly simple law is fraught with complex features. There is, for example, a "profit-sales ratio," which means that the man in business is concerned with seeing that his profits increase in proportion to his sales volume, under penalty of succumbing to more efficient competitors. If the wages and salaries he pays out go up, he must raise his prices not merely in the amount needed to meet his added labor costs, but with a markup designed to keep the overall structure of his business in balance. The pie may increase in size, but the proportional slice that goes to each participant (labor, materials, taxes, stockholders, etc.) must be kept approximately the same.

In the case of the investor or saver, there is a similarly motivated tendency to pass from a form of investment with a lower yield to one with a higher yield (from a savings bank that pays 5 percent to a high-grade bond that pays 7 percent, for instance), simply because he needs more money to keep pace with inflation (this passage from a lower to a higher yield, incidentally, is known in financial circles by the highly technical name of "disintermediation"). The "incomes theory" gives rise to other interesting practices. We recall the days when most beer or soft-drink bottles were returnable for washing and reuse. With modern technology, it costs more to reuse old bottles than to "recycle" them; that is, grind them down to glass powder and then blow up the powder into brand-new bottles. But the saving of old bottles for recycling has not yet been made as attractive to the holder of the empty bottle as the two or three cents he used to get when it was reused. In the real estate field, there is a relatively new practice, whose legal aspects are now being considered, known as the "kicker." The lender of money for building purposes demands, in addition to his interest and the eventual return of his capital, a piece of the action; that is, of the profits of the real estate operation. Would this be the case if the economy were truly stable? From Britain comes the term "gazumping," said to be a borrowing from Yiddish *gezumph*, to describe the practice of raising the price of a house after a deposit has been paid.

There is occasional humor in finance, as where one writer went into the psychological effects of describing a 36 percent decline in a company's earnings by saying that earnings had "declined" that much, while another report was to the effect that earnings had "plunged" that much. There is the use of "medi-recession," said to be intermediate between "mini-recession" and "maxi-recession." There is the "creditability gap" by which one financial writer describes the seemingly contradictory practices of the banks of advocating a rise in the primary interest rates to discourage excessive spending, while at the same time investing millions of dollars in advertising to promote customer borrowing (particularly of the credit card variety) at the inflated credit rates. Lastly, there is the very large family of terms involved in production and distribution techniques to which Barton refers in his *New Yorker* article: "incentive schemes," "labor productivity," "statistical quality control," "standard costing," "total marketing," "positioning our brand in the market-place," "brand acceptance," "consumer franchise," "synergistic effects of disparate affiliates," "planning gaps," "market segmentation," "corporate responsibility," etc. It is possible that all these terms have specific and legitimate meanings, but it would be imprudent to bank too much on it. Fairly clear and well-chosen, on the other hand, is the use of the term "anationals" to refer to big international companies operating in many countries under the respective laws of each nation.

As against all these abstrusities, there is the rollicking use of nicknames on the Stock Exchange, as where the good traders refer to Continental Can as "Zsa Zsa Gabor."

16

What's New in Euphemisms and Coinages?

When a dogcatcher is renamed "animal welfare officer" and a garbage collector who separates refuse into what is and is not reusable is labeled a "garbologist" (what happened to the old-time "ragpicker"?), people begin to wonder how euphemistic you can get without tripping over your own toes. When a cow barn is equipped with canned music, then styled a "milking parlor" or "lounging shed," and the residence of a Texas pastor is described as a "pastorium," the suspicion deepens that modern society is far too given to the art of double-talk. At this point, euphemistic jokes begin to circulate, as when a "gentleman" is defined as a "wolf with patience" (with the added notice that a true gentleman never uses the word "gentleman"); or a member of the lower echelons of society is made to state that he started out in life as a simple bum, but now he is a "hard-core unemployed"; or female breasts are redefined as the "upper frontal superstructure"; or the word "unpleasant" is changed to "rebarbative," a word that entered English in 1892 from French, where it had existed for centuries with the original meaning of "beard to beard," or facing the enemy, something that is irritating and unpleasant.

That the phenomenon of euphemism is not specifically American is proved by the recent British change of what used to be known as boardinghouses to "guest houses." The British, however, drew the line at the suggestion that the landladies should be restyled "hostesses." This, said the critics, would lend itself to too much confusion, in view of airline, bus, and train hostesses.

That euphemisms are at times surprisingly ancient, and not the modern innovations we think, was recently indicated by a bit of research we did for a correspondent. She objected to the twin euphemisms "pass away" and "pass on" for "to die," and wondered what their origin might be. A survey of numerous dictionaries and manuals of usage brought several interesting items to light. According to the British Oxford Dictionary, it all started in early Middle English with "pass," now described as archaic and dialectal, but still used by Shakespeare in *King Lear*. This seemingly gave rise to "pass away," also placed in the Middle English period (*passen away* is the Middle English form; neither "pass" nor "pass away" could have arisen as euphemisms before the Norman Conquest, as "pass" is a loan-word from Norman-French). "Pass away" is described by all major dictionaries (Oxford, Random House, Webster Third, American Heritage) as thoroughly in use, and Webster even has a quote from Virginia Woolf. The case is not so clear for "pass on," which does not appear in Oxford or American Heritage, and is given, without comment, by Webster Third and Random House. The fact that Oxford does not mention it would seem to point to rather recent origin, possibly American (Oxford does give "pass out," "pass up," the second labeled American). The dictionaries of slang (Partridge, Wentworth and Flexner) mention neither usage, indicating that they do not consider "pass away" and "pass on" as slang forms. The manuals of usage are completely silent on the two euphemisms (this is true of Fowler, Follett, Nicholson, Laird, Bernstein) save for Bergen Evans, who mentions both, and describes them as "vulgarities." French uses *passer* as a rather high-flown euphemism for "to die" (this accounts for "pass" in Middle English); the other Romance languages do not. The vulgar Italian *Passa via!* means literally "Pass away!" but is used with the meaning of "Get out of here!" "Scram!" not "Drop dead!"

Some euphemisms are both traditional and accidental, as when conservationists speak of "thinning out" herds of deer, elk, and other wildlife. The intention may be good, but the animal who is thinned out does not normally appreciate it. In like manner, the lumber interests speak of "harvesting" trees, while the conservationists speak of "butchering" them. Other euphemisms are novel and contradictory, but still purely accidental, as when a weathercaster describes the day as "oppressively mild." Some are deliberate in a good cause, as when it is proposed that to draw more people to the field of automotive mechanics, the mechanic be dignified with the title of "automobile engineer," or "engine redesigner," or "vehicular consultant." In Washington, the Senate bootblack is known as the "footwear maintenance engineer." In the same spirit, New York's gypsy cab drivers demanded for themselves and their vehicles the more flattering titles of "non-medallion" cabs and cabbies.

A few euphemisms are downright weasely, as when the news media described the alleged Mafia gang war that culminated in the shooting of Joe Colombo as a "struggle for preeminence in the Italian community."

One gem comes from the United Nations, where a study group proposed the elimination of words said to carry racist implications. Among the condemned words were "backward," "pagan," "native," "primitive," "tribe," "underdeveloped," "race," "savage," and "colored." Speaking of "tribe," a Nigerian member of the study group stated: "How an ethnic group with two or ten million people in East or West Africa, with a parliamentary government, can be described as a tribe, and not the Irish, the Scots, the Welsh, the French, or the English, still baffles the non-European."

It would be idle to deride these complaints on the ground that they betoken excessive sensitivity. It is a fact that some of them at least have come to convey, right or wrong, a derogatory or at least negative sense (the "heathen Chinese" was widely circulated in the West during the period of widespread missionary zeal). Yet some of them are precise, and it is hard to see how they could be replaced. How else to describe certain groups in New Guinea and the forests of the Amazons except as "backward," "underdeveloped," and "primitive," though one might add "by our western standards"? "Tribe" is a word that has its roots in ancient Rome (see page 87); it is inappropriate to describe a nation like the Zulus, but can logically be applied to one of its local subdivisions. "Savage" might well be avoided, in view of the inherent savagery occasionally displayed by Europeans or Americans, while "native" means born on the spot, and one can be a "native" Frenchman as well as a "native" Basuto. "Colored" used to be the American euphemism for "black" when one didn't want to say "Negro." It is differently used in South Africa, to refer to groups that are neither white nor black, like the numerous East Indians. Come to think of it, "white" is woefully imprecise, since most "whites" are ruddy, sallow, or tanned.

Taboo words in our own American society are contrasted with other words that have lost at least part of their taboo content in a *New York Times* article by Laura Z. Hobson. The topic of her discussion is which "offensive" words are and are not used in CBS's program *All in the Family*. Perceptively, the author of *Gentleman's Agreement* brings out the fact that in this supposed spoof on bigotry, Jews may be referred to as "Yids," "Yentas," "Hebes," "Chosen People," but not as "Kikes" or "Sheenies"; that while blacks may be described as "spades," "coons," "black beauties," or "jungle bunnies," the word "niggers" is never used; that while it is all right to refer to Italians as "Dagoes," the word "Mafia" is *verboten*. "Polacks" for Poles and "Spics" for Puerto Ricans seem permissible. She wonders whether CBS, or the show's script writer, may not have made up a little "list of forbidden words" deemed too offensive even for what purports to be an "honest" if hilarious portrayal of religious, racial, and ethnical intolerance. She also wonders (and so do we) whether young viewers should be exposed to any part of the vocabulary of bigotry with the concomitant temptation to use it in their own speech and thoughts.

One "Word in the Family" that Mrs. Hobson seems to take no exception to is "Dingbat," the "lovable bigot's" normal term of address for his long-suffering wife. This term, which fails to appear in Oxford, is defined by Webster Third, Random House, and American Heritage as a printer's type ornament similar to a star, designed to draw attention to an opening sentence or show a break between paragraphs; a small object to be thrown; a gadget. To find it applied to a person, we have to refer to Wentworth and Flexner, who describe it as a synonym for hobo, in student use since 1948, and also a derogatory term for an Italian,

Chinese, or "a woman other than one's own sister or mother," which affords our hero some justification (save for the derogatory note). "Meathead," which Archie Bunker reserves for his son-in-law, is described as in widespread use since 1949. "Yenta" is defined in American Heritage as Yiddish for gossipy woman, with possible derivation from Italian *gentile;* but Wentworth and Flexner give "yentzer" as Yiddish for cheater, untrustworthy character, derived from *yentz,* to fornicate, and in use since 1930. Confusing, to say the least. One additional term heard on America's favorite TV program is "labonza," meaning the posterior, which is attributed to Jackie Gleason and is said to have been first used in 1955.

Euphemism is at its best in the advertising world, where, as we have seen, it is part of the stock in trade. Philip L. Dougherty, writing in *The New York Times,* points out that euphemism is in constant use not merely in the advertising itself, but also within the agency, and gives samples with appropriate translations: "The new agency indicated a thorough understanding of our problem" really means: "They agreed to take a 12 instead of a 15% commission." The client's request for "the best of schlock" is interpreted as referring to cheap, gaudy, eye-catching material instead of high-quality, glossy advertising (see page 25).

Coinages run all the way from modern reintroduction into U.S. usage of Middle English expressions, like the "soring" of the feet of Tennessee walking horses to make them prance more gracefully, to the "condomarinium" which combines two other recent coinages, "condominium" and "marina," to express the ultramodern concept of land-based luxury hotels, resorts, and yachts.

Only occasionally do we get an expression that springs

full-grown from the brain of Minerva, so to speak, like the "khulyagus" coined by Dr. Gerald Phillips, of Penn State, in accordance with his principle that if a word-launching could spring up simultaneously in both Pennsylvania and Montana, it would have a good chance to achieve common usage. Unfortunately, he forgot to give "khulyagus" a meaning, so the press comment is that it is a wonderful word that can mean anything you want it to mean.

The majority of recent coinages are of the portmanteau variety, like the "Mexicancellation" that refers to a Mexican divorce, or "satisficer," which combines "satisfy" and "suffice," or "bratitude," said to have been coined by a school principal to describe the outstanding quality of his more recalcitrant pupils. "Growsy" has occurred to someone as a blend of "grumpy" and "drowsy," as when you are first awakened by the alarm clock.

The Eastman Kodak Company both reports and advocates (the latter for picture-taking purposes) a revival of the seventeenth-century "shunpiking," which means taking the backroads to avoid turnpike tolls. Bishop Fulton Sheen definitely states that he is coining a word he proposes to use, "staurophobia" (literally, "fear of the cross"), then defines it as "fear of discipline, penance, restraint, fasting, taking up the cross, and expiation of one's sins: definitely a major characteristic of our historical period." The elegant "legemoron" (Latin *legere*, "to read," plus Greek *moros*, "foolish") is offered by Paula J. Hessler, of Phoenix, Arizona, for "a legitimate word in print which is perceived by the reader to be nonsense or meaningless, or to have a possible double meaning" ("molester" read as "mole-ster," "molestation" as "mole-station," "misled" as "miss'led," or, for an amateur etymologist, to derive "helicopter" from *heli*, "sun," plus *copter*, "wing," instead of from *helico*, "spiral," plus *pter*, "wing").

"Sno-fari" is a word that has arisen in snowmobile circles to indicate hunting from a snowmobile. "Newtique" is the designation for some art shops that have put together "antique" and "boutique." "Underdeprived" gilds the lily, like the earlier "irregardless" that borrowed its prefix from "irrespective." Someone offered "splendacious" ("splendid" crossed with "mendacious," perhaps?), and someone else carried it on to "spendacious," to be applied to agencies that spend the taxpayer's money and lie about it. Still another genius labeled black-eyed peas "atrocious," because etymologically, "black-eyed" is exactly what "atrocious" means (*ater,* "black," plus *oculus,* "eye"). A black word-coiner, speaking of Rockefeller's projected state building to be erected in Harlem, spoke of Whitey's "tricknology," based on technology. That the process of coining is not restricted to English is shown by the ingenious Italian creation of *pelitecnico* applied to a barber (*pelo* is a hair, and *tecnico* is a technician; there is a link with the legitimate *politecnico,* which means a polytechnical institute). "Death clean" is reported from Utah to describe the state in which a conscientious housewife wants her house to be if death should suddenly strike her.

One of the most prolific coiners of words is Professor Edward Mishan of the London School of Economics. In one breath he gives us "growthmen" (for economists who advocate growth), "illfare" (the opposite of "welfare" as used in "Department of Health, Education, and Welfare"), "uglifying," "Newfanglia" (an imaginary region of England), and, best of all, "bads" as the opposite of "goods" for merchandise.

One somewhat weird but highly ingenious series of coinages, accompanied by suitable designs, is offered in the pages of the *Christian Science Monitor* for November 6, 1971, by Joseph Selame, a professional designer of artistic trademarks: "Got" is defined as "somewhere along the line —my forefather did mighty fine" (the accompanying design is of a man with a protruding paunch and a fat cigar in his mouth); "Nogot" is "He got his. Will I get mine?" and shows two lean and hungry figures; "Poligot" is "peace at any price, taken out of gross before taxes, of course"; and "Antigot" (figures with upraised clenched fists) is "Peace so dear—Revolution so near." There are all sorts of "tek" combinations, such as "politek," "teletek," "hipnotek," "robotek," "computek," and "creditek" (the last doesn't look too much like a credit card, but says: "Borrow, borrow—Pay back tomorrow"). The rest of the story, which undertakes to describe all the various characters that people the earth, is contained in Selame's book *So We Spin*, which should make fascinating reading.

If I may be permitted a suggested coinage, it is "nyes," for "no-yes" or "yes and no," which has the additional bonus of an international flavor (Russian *nyet* plus English "yes").

One picturesque type of coinage that has recently drawn attention is the so-called "Hash-House Greek" of *New York Times* writer Dan Carlinsky (no Greek at all, but highly imaginative restaurant English). After reminding us that what is a "hero sandwich" in New York is a "hoagy" in Philadelphia or Birmingham, a "grinder" in Hartford, a "poor boy" in New Orleans (he might have added the Kentucky–West Virginia–southern Ohio area), a "torpedo" in San Diego, an "Italian sandwich" in Louisville, a "Cuban sandwich" in Miami, he goes on to offer some coinages of very ancient vintage: "Adam and Eve on a raft" for poached eggs on toast; "wreck 'em" if you want them scrambled; "black and white" for a chocolate soda with vanilla ice cream; "over" or "up" for fried eggs. Then he goes on to cite innovations: "all the way" for either with all condiments or well done; "bucket of mud" for a dish of chocolate ice cream; "crowd" for three orders of an item ("two is company," etc.); "hail" for ice (logical, since "ice" has become the slang for diamonds); "let it walk" or "on wheels" for an order to take out ("walking order" has been in use since 1945; "on wheels" has the more customary meaning of "with enthusiasm" or the other old slang phrase, "with bells on"); "spot" for a cup of tea, following British usage.

Readers of his article, of course, immediately came forward with additions: "burn the British" for toasted English muffins; "high and dry" for no condiments; "shmeer" for layer of cream cheese on a bagel.

One curious feature of Hash-House Greek is the use of certain numerals with symbolical value: "nineteen" for banana split; "thirteen" for "watch out, the boss is around" (this is reminiscent of the ancient "23-skiddoo" for modern "scram"); "eighty-one" for a glass of water; "ninety-one" for a glass of seltzer. Wentworth and Flexner report the use of "eighty," "eighty-one," and "eighty-two" in connection with water since the 1930s, but have no suitable explanation, and fail to mention the other numbers.

Linguistic creativity can extend even to the coining of imaginary laws of nature. Inspired by *Parkinson's Law* and the *Peter Principle,* possibly even by my *Physical Law of the Cussedness of Inanimate Objects*, a man named J. Lyons, owner of a cooperative apartment, came out with the "Rule of Twice" (work out your estimate of what it will cost you and how long it will take for your building and redecorating, then multiply everything by two, because you can bet your B.P.'s that it will be twice as costly and take twice as long as estimated).

The opposite of coinages that try to get into the language, and sometimes succeed, is the much smaller number of words that fall into desuetude, and receive the labels of "obsolescent," "obsolete," ultimately "archaic" in our more comprehensive dictionaries. Lists of such words have occasionally appeared. It is seldom, however, that attention is called to them directly as they are in the process of obsolescence. One such word, mentioned in *The New York Times,* October 31, 1971, by writers Betty Comden and Adolph Green, is "winsome," about which they say: "Words like winsome have fallen into disuse in 1971." This statement is of value in that it furnishes future literary historians with a precise point of departure for a process of desuetude. More should be offered, but while words impinge upon our consciousness by their appearance, they seldom mark themselves as conspicuous by their absence.

The productive prefixes and suffixes described at length in *Words in Sheep's Clothing* continue to be productive. "Rock-in" for a rock festival was added to the *-in* group, being paralleled by "sick-out" (a phenomenon said to appear commonly in airlines). The large *-nik* family was augmented by "folknik" for a fancier of folk music, "smutnik" for one who likes smut, "kaputnik" for someone or something doomed to failure, even "boatnik," used as the title of a recent film (*The Boatniks*). Further advice on "subbotnik" definitely confirms its origin from *subbota,* Russian for "Saturday." The institution of the "subbotnik," a holiday of labor, when the entire population turns out to prune bushes, repair streets, and wash windows, was inaugurated by Lenin in 1919, and subbotniks have been held from time to time to rally the people around specific events.

This is part of what the *San Antonio Express* calls "creeping suffixism." "Remedy" leads to "remedial" (as in remedial reading), and that in turn to "remediation," while a supporting or sustaining drive becomes a "sustentation" drive. "How can we sustentain a word like that?" inquires the editor, unconsciously producing what the linguists would call a back-formation.

17

"Beautiful" and "Ugly" Words

Periodically, polls are conducted to determine what the speakers consider "beautiful" words from a purely esthetic point of view and, conversely, which words they view as "ugly." As far back as 1932 Wilfred Funk offered a list of "the ten most beautiful words in the language," which turned out to be "dawn," "hush," "lullaby," "murmuring," "tranquil," "mist," "luminous," "chimes," "golden," and "melody." This was countered by a list of the ten "ugliest" words, selected by the National Association of Teachers of Speech: "phlegmatic," "crunch," "flatulent," "cacophony," "treachery," "sap," "jazz," "plutocracy," "gripe," and "plump." A contemporary British list of "beautiful" choices included "carnation," "azure," "moon," "heart," "silence," "shadow," and "April," while their "ugly" list, coinciding only in part with the American ("gripe," "jazz," "cacophony" were in both), added "scram," "guzzle," "mange," "swell," and "spinach." At a considerably later date, J. Donald Adams published his own "ugly" choices in his *Sunday Times Book Review* column. Here were found "crepuscular," "beautician," "pulchritudinous," "polygamous," "snaggle-toothed," "pneumococcus," "adumbrate," and "pococuranteism," indicating a preoccupation with lengthy and little-used forms. *The Glen Ridge* (New Jersey) *Paper*, in an editorial of October 22, 1971, condemns the Swedish imported word "Omsbudsman" as "awkward and unpronounceable to English speakers."

One could say that this is all a matter of individual taste. Vincent Canby, in one of his movie reviews, states that he finds "fungus" beautiful and "moon" a "dumb" word, and that while he likes "exquisite" with stress on the initial syllable, he finds it flat when stressed on the second, and a downright fraud when spelled out in neon. He adds, however, that he goes by sound, not by meaning—which is the crux of the issue. In the earlier lists, it is fairly evident that a good deal of the choice depended on meaning rather than sound, though even then someone remarked that he found "cellar-door" a beautiful word.

One might say that to assure the validity of the esthetic test, the words submitted should be from languages unknown to the people polled. Even so, it would be difficult to divorce the foreign, unknown word from possible similarity of sound and consequent association in meaning with other words in a language that one knows.

Since I am acquainted with too many languages for my own good, at least for this particular purpose, I may set forth a list of my own which is international, leaving it to the reader to judge whether I was unconsciously guided by meaning. A beautiful word to me is Japanese *yuki** (snow;

---

* Yuki (YOO-kee); sneg (SNYEK); dozhd' (DAWZHD); skazka (SKAHZ-kuh); ptitsa (PTEET-suh); izba (eez-BAH); tachanka (tah-CHAHN-kuh) domovina (doh-moh-VEE-nah); thalassa (THAH-lahs-sah); thanatos (THAH-nah-tohs); Elohim (eh-loh-HEEM); shalom

but not its Russian counterpart *sneg,* or, for that matter, Russian *dozhd',* rain); on the other hand, I like Russian *skazka* (fairy tale), *ptitsa* (bird), *izba* (hut), *tachanka* (horse-drawn machine gun); Serbo-Croatian *domovina* (native land); Greek *thalassa* (sea), but also *thanatos* (death); Hebrew *Elohim* (Lord) and *shalom* (peace; the normal word of greeting); Hungarian *viszontlátásra* (good-bye); Swahili *kubembeleza* (caress); Zulu *inkosikasi* (chieftainess) and *Amazulu* (the Zulu nation); Turkish *ateş* (fire). Despite its caressing meaning (treasure, beloved) I find German *Schatz* ugly. I love Latin place-names and other words ending in *-umnus* (*Clitumnus, autumnus*), but the ending is Etruscan. For place-names, I find beautiful Chinese *Shantung* (mountain-east) and Hindi *Rajasthan* (land of kings). I love the ancient Avestan name of the "Wise Spirit," *Ahura-mazda,* but not its later Persian form, *Ormazd.*

Coming back to English, three of my favorite gripes are "nitty-gritty," "goo" (or "gooey"), and "guts"; but here, how to dissociate sound from meaning? Even "nitty-gritty" stems from "nit"and"grit."

To try to settle the issue, I asked a highly literate group of graduate students of English at Seton Hall University to give me, individually and without collusion, their lists of five beautiful and five ugly words, along with five coinages of words they would like to see in the language and five words they thought might profitably be dropped from the language. In the matter of cacophonous and euphonious

---

(shah-LOHM); viszontlátásra (VEE-sont-lah-tahsh-ruh); kubembeleza (koo-bem-beh-LEH-zah); inkosikasi (een-koh-see-KAH-see); Amazulu (ah-mah-ZOO-loo); ateş (ah-TESH); Schatz (SHAHTS); Clitumnus (klee-TOOM-noos); autumnus (ow-TOOM-noos); Shantung (SHAHN-doong); Rajasthan (RAH-jahst-han); Ahura-mazda (ah-HOO-rah-MAHZ-dah); Ormazd (ohr-MAHZD).

words, they were cautioned to go by sound rather than by meaning; but in their coinages and discards they were free to combine both.

In a group of eighteen students, it was interesting to see how little coincidence there was. Among ugly words, five chose "cacophony" (or "cacophonous" or "cacophonic"), two selected "cantankerous," two "cackling." "Plump," selected by two as ugly, was listed as beautiful by one. "Serendipity" was among the beautiful choices of four, "peace" (or "peaceful") of three, "lavender," "silence," "murmur," "whisper," "willow," "low," "love" (or "lovely") of two each. "Ain't," selected by one as cacophonic, was chosen by two more as among desirable discards from use. Other proposed word dropouts, winning two votes apiece, were "awful," "pretty," "great" (in adverbial use, as in "pretty good" or "Great!"), and "hippie." There were no coincidences in coinages, but the suffixes -*itis* and -*phobia* appeared eight and two times, respectively (but only three voters contributed the eight cases of -*itis,* and a single voter the two cases of -*phobia*). The -*ous* suffix appeared five times among words to be dropped, with three contributors. This suffix also appeared in six words described as ugly-sounding, and in seven described as beautiful, but was used only twice in coinages.

Ugly words showed a tendency to be monosyllabic and of native origin ("loot," "snooze," "retch," "puke," "creep," "botch," "bog," "fink," "snort," "scratch," "crack," "gut," "pick," "wrench," "pap," "dredge," "jazz," "jive," "gripe," "won't," "brat," "ow," "can't"). This was only partly true of candidates for discard ("waste," "goon," "hark," "gang," "swell," "junk," "crap," "slurp").

Typical of cacophonous words where the choice may have been determined by the meaning were "raunch," "rowdy," "grinding," "gravel," "obesity," "cuckold," "crazy," "braggart," "gangster," "blackguard," "hackneyed," "rambunctious," "polygamy," "scuttle," "oxymoron," "poltergeist," "vitiate," "disturb," "exclude," "garbage" (and "garbologist"), "pimple," "jalopy." But meaning could hardly have been a factor in "moody," "sanctity," "palatable," "rectify," "bosom," "pulchritudinous," "aggrandize," "macadam," "prototype," "paleontologist," "miscellaneous," "dexterity," "purple," "communicative," Personal factors of taste may have gone into "khaki," "pugilist," "iconoclastic," "pyx," "sergeant," "stampede," "onion," "potato," and "colonel."

For euphonious words, there was a fair sprinkling of foreign forms: *Zeitgeist, Weltanschauung, anthropos, Lorelei.* Polysyllabic forms of obviously foreign and learned origin were numerous: "sonorous," "epidermal," "collaborate," "resilient," "mellifluous," "lugubrious," "euphoria," "eulogy," "platitude," "aphorism," "panorama," "evanescence," "spontaneous," "symphony," "caricature," "superfluous," "opalescence," "luminous," "scintillating," "nefarious," "tantalize." Words where the meaning may have played a part in the choice included "virtue," "sympathy," "vision," "softness," "sunny," "delightful," "leisure," "rustle," "soothe," "smooth," "sensible," "ocean," "melody," "golden," "tranquil," "calm," "dove." It could hardly have entered into "windfall," "highwire," "moll," "mom," "mound," "fall," "may," "sigh," "fire," "mirror," "bewilderment," "sheer," "wind," "flow," "crystal," "billowing," "eerie," "languish." "Conservative" may have been due to a subjective factor, as also the proper adjective "Roman" and the proper name "Millicent."

Among proposed discards, meaning may have had to do with "Lesbian," "lukewarm," "roundabout," "momism," "humanoid," "boorish," "alack," "alas," "mongoloid," "gout," "moron," "imbecile," "vegetable" (referring to a person), "contumelious," "censorious," "niggardly," "banal," "miscarriage," "mishap," "blemishes." Personal or cultural factors may have influenced "age of reason," "Dark Ages," "writ of habeas corpus," "executive," "poetess," "authoress." Preoccupation with language standards and opposition to gobbledegook and affected talk are evidenced by "supercalifragilisticexpalidocious" (does it really exist?), "antidisestablishmentarianism" (this one does), "angeliferous," "colossal," "whereby," "heretofore," "fantastic," "sandwiched," "mastermind," "darling," "marvelous," and, on the seamier side of the language, "itsy-bitsy," "beatnik," "teeny-bopper," "crap," "ma'am," "gee whiz," the conflict between "flammable" and "inflammable," the one between "burn up" and "burn down," "damn," and "shit." The reasons for "roundabout," "transpire," "staircase" or "stairway," "pocketbook," "fecund," "enormous," "amalgamate," "elegant," "idiot," escape us.

A true element of inventiveness and imagination was displayed in the coinage of words deemed desirable for inclusion in the language. Here we find formation by suffixation ("examinitis," "teen-age-itis," "graduatitis," defined as "fear of graduating," "Twigginess," "blufferity," "cornballish," "competiphobia," "mutatophobia" (for "fear of change"), "moonomania," "panelology," "despocracy," "fadial" (for one who goes along with fads), "duplicuous," "think-in," "tantalization," "happiless." Formation by prefixation is exemplified by "nonself" (for a drug addict), "maliberated" (for an undesirable liberated female), "unwar" (a war fought without declaring it), "subsocialism" (the kind of socialism that pulls a nation under), "to smean" (to really mean). "Antipeacenik" shows both prefixation and suffixation. There are compressions and combinations: "yo," for yes-and-no, to be used by the undecided; "jackalong," one who moves jerkily in many directions, and "schlepalong," undefined by its creator; "duddy" (for "dark and bloody"; think of Kentucky as "the duddy ground"); "quave" (cool and suave); "gigandous" (gigantic-tremendous); "strates" (student demonstrators); "valnew" (value renewal, in Youth Culture); "slumsick"; "peacemate"; "stuvolt" (student revolt); "bosstard" (political boss); "fuzzmobile" (police car); "schoolbore" (one bored with school, or whose school is bored with him); "soulsection" (all-black class); "antiquidate"; "cupickle" (half-sour pickle); "sillicent" (empty-headed but attractive girl); "starkitecture (the UN building, perhaps?). A few are utter creations, with no seeming precedent: "gavonne" (undesirable person); "deven" (a man's love for a man, without homosexual overtones); "ferch" (a "gummy build-up on a guitar"); "pokercadipillar" (impish, naughty, but endearing child); "Johnny Chinkle" (figurine); "mavebrow" (long, winding path); "farkle" (young, clumsy, but nice); "gloving" (doing in secret). There is also a "permapress smile," a "boron" for a boring person, a "circumpointer" for one who beats around the bush, a "bopiner" for one who drops or bops in, a "junker" for a dope pusher, "summa cum lousy" for to graduate last in the class, "liberacide" for one who would destroy freedom, "taxic" for one suffering from overtaxation, "adiposeorrhea" for fat folds that overflow, and even a "dodifferentday" for a day on which you all agree to do something different from usual.

So goes a batch of creations that could well fit into our chapter on coinages. Also, quite a few of them display all the requisites for inclusion in a Weasel Word Dictionary, being politically or ideologically slanted. Who will say after this that our colleges don't turn out people who are able to think for themselves?

18

Usage and Abusage

Is the English language degenerating faster than it used to? Perhaps, if "degenerating" is the right word.

More and more the press media bring to us misspellings like "permissable," "tax deductable," "advisible," or "supercede" for "supersede," due to the fact that the ear tends to deceive both the eye and the memory of what was once, hopefully, learned. Yet there is etymological excuse (not quite justification) for "errors" of this type. Both -*abilis* and -*ibilis* are good Latin suffixes indicating something that is possible. They are confused in Latin; should it be altogether surprising to see them confused in English? The -*sede* of the "correct" "supersede" comes from the verb that means to sit, and the compound means to sit above. The -*cede* of the "incorrect" "supercede" comes from a verb that means to step, and the compound means to step above. Either works out well semantically.

There are cases of alternate spelling, like "busing" and

"bussing," the first of which lends itself to being pronounced like "using," the second to confusion with kissing. Hoary rules of grammar are openly disregarded on TV (not merely "like a cigarette should," but also, at the opening of every *Star Trek* program, "to boldly go where no man has gone before," with the infinitive split right down the middle). Open defiance is flaunted at puristic viewers: "What do you want, good grammar or good taste?" Some of us might settle for a little of both.

Having survived "coffee-er coffee," "peanuttiest" and "macaroniest," we are now faced with "Survival of the Hippest," the title of an article by Don Heckman in the theatrical section of *The New York Times*. This arouses a further doubt: Is it meant to be "hippie-hippier-hippiest" or "hip-hipper-hippest"?

"Who" and "whom" are hopelessly confused, even in the mouths of lawyers: not only "Who did you see?" but also "Whom do you believe is guilty?" The redundant conjunction "that" gets more and more redundant, as when Secretary of State Rogers comes out with: "We think *that* if a peaceful settlement is not worked out in the foreseeable future, *that* a very dangerous situation will develop."

Side by side with vulgar innovations, there is a curious return to obsolescent words that goes hand in hand with the return of *No, No, Nanette.* Such long-discarded forms as "gazebo" and "lallapaloosa" are brought back into circulation, mainly by the advertising media (but the use of "whilom" in the sense of "former" stems rather from the field of journalism). There is a distortion of foreign words and expressions, as when "Mafia" is made the anagram for "Mothers and Fathers of Italian Ancestry," and "Cosa Nostra" is reshaped into "Kosher Nostra." New foreignisms are brought into the language and immediately given naturalization papers, like the Greek *taberna* and *ouzo,* or the Yiddish *chutzpah* and *kvetch* (the last two are such recent additions to the language that they do not appear in the older dictionaries, and have barely made it into the ones published after 1966; *taberna* is really a Greek borrowing from Latin, and is suspected of being originally Etruscan; *kvetch* is a Yiddish borrowing from German *quetschen*, to complain).

Another Yiddish-Hebraic term which has long appeared in both British and American English (all dictionaries carry it, save, strangely, American Heritage; and Wentworth and Flexner, while reporting it, do not even bother to give its date of entry into American slang) is the form that currently appears as "momser" (more properly, it should be spelled "mamser" or "mamzer"). Oxford reports it as coming into English in 1562, from the Vulgate (Book of Deuteronomy), and stemming from Hebrew *mamzēr*. It was recently discussed at length in a correspondence to the *Los Angeles Times* from Tel Aviv, where the *mamzerim* (loosely translated as bastards) present a problem. In American Yiddish usage, the term commonly means a sponger, a nuisance, one who is too demanding. But the original Biblical meaning, rendered only imperfectly by "bastard," is not one born out of wedlock (against whom there are no religious sanctions), but one born to a married woman and not fathered by her lawful husband. The strict Rabbinical law provides for divorce and remarriage, but the divorce must be pronounced by a Rabbinical court. Hence, one born to a woman who obtained a civil divorce, legal in her country of residence, and later remarried is a "bastard" in the Rabbinical sense, and forbidden even unto the tenth generation from entering the congregation of the Lord or being married by a rabbi (the only type of marriage permitted in Israel among people of the Jewish faith). What to do, then, with Jews entering from abroad with second wives or husbands who are legally recognized everywhere but in Israel? The "Case of the Mamzerim" is now under deep consideration. For popular U.S. usage, however, the equivalence of "momser" and "bastard" as a term of obloquy, without religious overtones, still persists.

There is a rather frequent use of foreign greetings and leave-takings: Italian *ciao* and *arrivederci,* coupled with Jack O'Brian's *tanti auguri* (best wishes); German *auf Wiedersehen;* Spanish *adiós;* French *adieu* and *au revoir;* but the French forms are fairly traditional in English. Other foreign terms creep into the more cultural segment of the language, like the Russian *Amerikanisty,* which is the Soviet counterpart of our "Kremlinologists"; the *Amerikanisty,* experts on "Amerika," haunt the halls of the new American Institute in Moscow, and keep tabs on what we do and think.

But all this is, in a sense, the small change of the field of usage. The real questions about American usage are generally raised by foreigners. There is, for example, the case of an extremely competent Japanese translator, Hideaki Yamashita, who also happens to be director of the Department of International Affairs of the Tokyo Stock Exchange. Setting out to translate Stan Sauerhaft's *The Merger Game,* he had little trouble with the financial jargon, but was stumped by the more popular idioms. What was the meaning, he inquired, of "psychedelic banana split"? (For American readers who don't know, either, it's a highly overdone, visually exotic image.) What is the meaning of "the cat's meow"? Of "the biggest and most expensive egg since the Edsel"? Who are the "Green Bay Packers"? What is a "Wellesley girl"? Where is "East Lynne"?

Or take a query received by this writer from a Japanese professor of English at Aichigakuin University in Nagoya,

Japan, who wants to be enlightened on several very delicate points of current American usage. Some of the issues are easily settled; but others are so subtle that I again called on my English graduate students at Seton Hall for help. The replies here summarized represent a consensus of expert opinion:

1. Q. Should a university professor be referred to as Professor, Doctor, or Professor Doctor?

   A. Doctor is reserved for one who holds the Ph.D. degree, whether or not he teaches, and at any level; Professor for one who holds academic teaching rank (Assistant Professor, Associate Professor, full Professor) at a college or university, whether or not he holds a doctoral degree. If he is entitled to both titles, use either. Normally, they are seldom combined in American usage, in the form illustrated by *Herr Professor Doktor Soundso,* favored by German, or *Dottor Professor Cavaliere Tal dei Tali,* current in Italian.

2. Q. Is the plural "handkerchieves" in current use in America?

   A. It is listed as secondary and archaic in Webster Third and fails to appear in the other dictionaries, including even the British Oxford. In practice, no American would be inclined to use it.

3. Q. Which is preferable: (a) I can't help feeling sorry for him; (b) I cannot choose but feel sorry for him; (c) I cannot but feel sorry for him; (d) I can't help but feel sorry for him?

   A. "I can't help feeling sorry for him" is by far the preferred form. "I can't help but feel sorry for him" is criticized by some authorities, but is in widespread use in the United States; less so in Britain. The other two expressions are somewhat archaic and formal.

4. Q. What is the distinction, if any, between "can't," "cannot," and "can not"?

   A. "Can't" and "cannot" are interchangeable, with "cannot" perhaps a little more emphatic. "Can not" is described by the British Oxford as current, but "cannot" is said to be "the usual modern way of spelling can not." The consensus is that it is acceptable, but as a sort of strongly emphatic way of rendering "can't."

5. Q. Which is preferable, "You can do it, can you not?" or "You can do it, can't you?"

A. "Can you not" is quite acceptable, but again strongly emphatic.

6. Q. Is "on account of I keep in shape" correct?

A. "On account of" followed by a clause is definitely substandard, and the literary quotes cited by the Japanese professor are of fictional characters obviously not too well educated. Nevertheless, the construction is in widespread use among such people.

7. Q. Is "at 12:30 o'clock" normal?

A. "At 12 o'clock" is normal. "At 12:30 o'clock" may be either very formal, as in a wedding invitation, or faintly substandard. Most of us would tend to avoid it, and use "at 12:30 P.M." or "at 12:30 in the afternoon."

8. Q. What is the difference between "to be good at" and "to be good in"?

A. This is a difficult one to answer. It has been suggested that there may be a distinction based on whether a single word or a word-group follows ("He is good in French"; "He is good at expressing himself in French"); or that one is good at an individual activity, but good in activities calling for collaboration ("He is good at expressing his point of view"; "He is good in organizing social activities"); or that one is good at an action, but good in a pursuit or calling ("He is good at tennis"; "He is good in social work"). The phrases involved in the two expressions are so highly idiomatic that they baffle classification. One has to go by ear.

9. Q. Which is more usual: "making an impression on someone" or "giving an impression of," "an impression on," "an impression that" (followed by a clause)?

A. "Making an impression on someone" is equivalent to

impressing someone. One gives the impression (rather than "an impression") of being angry, or the impression that he is motivated by altruistic motives. "To give an impression on" something is roughly equivalent to giving an informal opinion about something, but it is rare. Therefore: "He made a very favorable impression on me," equivalent to "He impressed me very favorably"; "He gave me his impression of what had happened."

10. Q. Which is correct: "to knock the door," "to knock at the door," "to knock on" or "upon the door"?

A. "To knock the door" is incorrect unless an adverb follows ("He knocked the door down") or one uses "knock," somewhat colloquially, in the sense of to belittle someone ("He knocked the police"; "Don't knock it till you've tried it"). "To knock at the door" is more usual, but "to knock on the door" is both permissible and current.

11. Q. Which is preferable: "to type a letter on the typewriter"; "to write a letter on the typewriter"; "to write a letter with the typewriter"?

A. "To type a letter on the typewriter" is redundant. You either "type a letter" or "write a letter on the typewriter." "To write a letter with the typewriter" is faintly unidiomatic, though you might express your feelings with the typewriter.

The first of our Japanese queries is perhaps the one most likely to interest an American speaker, as distinguished from a foreign learner of the language. Helen Meyner, wife of New Jersey's former governor, once published an article entitled "Democracy's Passion for Pompous Titles," in which she stated that we have relinquished Kings, Queens, Lords, Earls, Marchionesses, Ladies, Dames, and Sirs, but we still have many, perhaps too many, substitutes. In proof whereof she produced Secretaries, Senators, Congressmen, Mayors, Judges ("Honorable," "the Honorable," and "Your Honor" might have appeared at this point), Reverends, Very Reverends, Bishops, and all military and academic ranks. The confusion caused by using "Doctor" for a Ph.D. in philosophy as well as for an M.D. was brought out (West Virginia usage would make it a "teach-doctor" vs. a "real doctor"). Mrs. Meyner advocates the use of plain Mr., Mrs., and Miss, which fits in quite well with the general French practice of avoiding titles and addressing everybody as *Monsieur, Madame, Mademoiselle.* Other languages, as we have seen, pile up titles. But then, to quote a saying from the tongue of the worst offenders, *"Paese che vai, usanza che trovi"* ("Country where you go, custom that you find," or, more idiomatically, "When in Rome, do as the Romans do").

19

Oddments and Endments*

Attention has repeatedly been called to the differences in usage between the British and the American segments of the English-speaking world. While most of these are of long standing, there are a few that seem of relatively recent origin.

One correspondent writing to *The New York Times* complains that at a British roadside gas station she made a major linguistic gaffe when she asked the lady in charge if she had a "rest room." The rather reluctant reply took the form of an offer to let her lie down for a while in her own bedroom until she felt better. When she explained what she really wanted, there was hospitable insistence that she use the bathroom in the house, as it was "prettier" than the one

---

* For the title of this chapter I am indebted to my friend and colleague Professor Robert A. Hall, Jr., of Cornell University, who used the expressions in describing, in a review, some of the contents of an earlier book of mine.

at the garage. It is a fact that my own inquiry for such a facility in a Stratford hotel was met with the information that the "cloak room" was on the left as you came in. Oddly, "cloak room" in the wanted sense does not appear in Oxford, though it is reported as a British usage in our own Random House. But "rest room," which all American dictionaries without exception carry, is nonexistent in the Oxford.

The British use of "turn-up" for what we would style an "upset" came at the time of the last British election that turned out the Labor cabinet. For what it may be worth to our feminine readers, it turns out that "pantaloon sheaths" is one of the British versions for our "pantyhose"; neither term has made it in any of our dictionaries, British or native. British "dustman" is normal for our garbage or sanitation man, or what has more recently been euphemized into a "debris disposal technician." There is a British abbreviated "demo" for demonstration, which has not yet crossed the ocean, and a keen observer notes that the British speaker normally says "just now" where the American would say "right now." Three interesting Australian variants are "jackeroo," "muster," and "glory book," respectively, for American cowboy, roundup, and hope chest. The last seems to have its origin in British slang "glory hole" to indicate a repository for useless objects.

In a TV interview with Robert Morley from London, Dick Cavett introduced the word "bum," with its divergence of meaning in British and American English. Whether this was deliberate or accidental was not made clear. What I tried to make clear to Mr. Cavett in a letter is that British "bum" and American "bum" are two separate words, with altogether different origins. The British word, going back to Middle English "bom," has always had the meaning of "buttocks," "bottom." The American word, of much more recent immigrant origin, goes back to German *bommeln*, "to loaf, dawdle, loiter," with a noun *Bummel*, meaning a "stroll" or "saunter," and a derivative *Bummler*, which means "idler," "loafer." Its first recorded appearance is in 1871, but it probably goes back to the days of heavy German immigration in the 1850s. There is a concurrent but less-used form, "bummer," of which American "bum" is probably a cut-down version. The Oxford English Dictionary, which gives "bum" in its British, but not its American acceptance, speculates that the Middle English word may have been derived from "bump." Our American dictionaries at least give both acceptances. The two words simply happen to coincide in form.

Another illustration of slang differences between Britain and America is offered by the (British) English translation of Feydeau's *There Is One in Every Marriage,* where one of the leading characters, referring to a hotel maid, is moved to utter the words: "Holy saddlebag, what a bit of bang-tail!" The meaning is fairly obvious, but I leave it to my readers to supply the proper American version.

The question of British or American priority in the use of special catchphrases occasionally bobs up. In his Christmas Greeting Letter of 1971–1972, Eric Partridge definitely proves British priority, not only for such expressions as "black's your eye" and "I'll have your guts for garters," which no American in his right mind would dream of contesting, but also for "hay for horses" (traced back to Swift in the early eighteenth century) and "Does your mother know you're out?" (1840, but crossing the Atlantic in the same year). He is in doubt about "I couldn't care less" (1940) and "I couldn't agree more" (1930). "I'll say it is" and "You can say that again" (or "twice") are conceded to be American, but are traced back to an earlier British "say it again." "That makes the two of us" is claimed to be originally British. Then there is "That'll be the day!" coined in 1918, with the variant "That'll be the bloody day!" (which definitely marks itself as British), with a reference perhaps to German *der Tag* (the day when Germany would attain her dream place in the sun). Some American linguists may rise to dispute some of these findings. What cannot be disputed, of course, is British priority to the English language as a whole.

Place-names in the news with curious features are "Mooncusser's Lane," in the vicinity of Cape Cod, and "Knockemstiff," in Ohio, southwest of Chillicothe, which is in the 1971 highway map despite the fact that it boasts a population of only fifty inhabitants. There is no indication as to the origin of either name.

There is also the news item about the little town of 'Taint, in Oviedo County, Florida, which became tired of negating its own existence and changed its name to Taintsville; also, the former Pekin, Maryland, which got confused with Pekin, Indiana, and reversed its name to Nikep for Post Office purposes (unlike 'Taint, it has a Nikep zip code, 21546).

It has been noted that there is a wider gap between English and American place-names than there is between the two general languages. One driving through the English Cotswolds, for instance, encounters the following sequence of names, which would be highly unlikely in the American countryside: Wroxton, Stow-on-the-Wold, Darlinscott, Chipping Campden, Winchcombe, Upper Swell, and Lower Slaughter. A few American place-names derive from English forms and demand quasi-British pronunciation, such as Dedham, Needham, Waltham, Framingham, and Worcester (pronounced "Wooster"). The British tendency to telescope place-names was recently illustrated by Woolfordisworthy, in Devonshire, locally pronounced "Woolsery."

The pronunciation of place-names generally follows local usage (the whim of the inhabitants), whatever their origin. It is therefore not too surprising to find Vincennes pronounced VIN-sense, Boisé BOY-zee, etc. I always shrink instinctively from LOW-die for Lodi and Pay-OH-lee for Paoli; but my finest hour came when I was being driven through western Kansas and saw the sign "Paola." "How is that locality pronounced?" I inquired of my driver. He looked at me strangely, then replied: "I know what's on your mind, but we prononunced it pay-OH-lah long before you Easterners had coined the term you use for graft."

In the matter of personal names, attention has been called to what a linguist would style syncopated forms now current in feminine first names: Barbra Streisand, Marlyn Mason, Ann-Margret. Their significance is not obvious, unless it is merely designed to impress with the unusual feature, which normally appears only in writing, and does not affect the spoken form (though Marlyn might lend itself to a pronunciation MAR-lin).

Attention has perhaps already been called to the fact that in similar-sounding first names and diminutive nicknames, the written suffix -y usually indicates a masculine possessor, while -ie indicates a feminine ("Billy," "Franky," "Johnny," as against "Billie," "Frankie," "Johnnie"). But this is far from universal: note "May," "Mae," both feminine; "Charley," "Charlie," both usually masculine. Lovable is "Aprille," with its spurious French feminine suffix.

When food names are appropriated from other languages, they do not always fare too well. Italian-style *salame cotto* is prominently displayed by one firm with the label "Cotto Salami" (two inaccuracies in as many words). And have you ever tried calling for German Löwenbräu beer by its properly pronounced name?

There is a curious use of names of foods as pet names for people which may one day cross the ocean and land among us. French *mon petit chou* (literally, my little cabbage) as a term of endearment is of long standing, as are Italian names of cheeses (*mozzarella, provolone,* etc.) for inferior card players. But now there is word from Italy to the effect that *polpettone* (meat loaf) and *supplì* (rice croquette) are pet names used by Sofia Loren to Carlo Ponti. How would "my Little Roast Beef" or "my Darling Oyster Stew" strike the American ear?

One animal term of endearment seems to have crossed the ocean the other way. Our "Pussycat" has received not a French translation, but a French spelling adaptation, and now appears as *Poussiquette*, which is altogether in accord with both French phonology and French orthography. We may expect it to recross the ocean in its new form, and to see it soon in the name of some French New York restaurant (Chez la Poussiquette).

French influence appears elsewhere than in pet names, often in a mildly sexual context, as one might expect. To refer to a woman's powdering her nose, one might use the French slang *se sucrer les fraises* ("to sugar one's strawberries"; but beware—if you omit the reflexive pronoun and say *sucrer les fraises,* "to sugar strawberries," it applies to a man, and means that he is in his dotage). *Oeufs sur le plat* ("fried eggs up") and *oranges à l'étalage* ("oranges on display") refer to that part of the feminine anatomy which is usually most prominent and eye-catching, save with Twiggy types. There is a reason why the French call their slang *langue verte* ("green language").

Another foreign importation is "brouhaha" (French,

probably from *bruit,* "noise," plus *ha-ha,* imitative of loud laughter, though Webster Third has a rather improbable Hebrew etymology, *bārūkh habbā',* "blessed he who enters," mentioned by no other dictionary). Oxford does not report it, indicating both recent and probably American usage, and neither Wentworth and Flexner nor any French dictionary consider it slang. It seems to be in the nature of a recent yet already obsolescent word, brought into use by journalists and critics. Another such word, older, and of Greek origin, is "peripatetic" (the "Peripatetic Turtle" sweater, advertised by Lord and Taylor).

It has been ruled by the courts that individuals are the arbiters of how their own family names should be pronounced and spelled; for instance, a *New York Times* correspondent and a movie producer both use Polish spellings in their family names of German origin, Szulc and Szwarc, and only a linguist knows that they are to be pronounced "Schultz" and "Schwarz." But family names are subject to pressure from the majority group the possessor happens to live among. This means that a name like Jones among Spanish speakers may easily turn into HOH-nays, while a Spanish name like de Jesús (day-hay-SOOS in Spanish pronunciation) comes out in a New York courtroom as dee-JEE-zus.

I normally shudder when I hear a baseball player's name rendered as koh-nig-lee-AH-roh in the newscast, when I know that the proper pronunciation of Conigliaro is koh-nee-LYAH-roh. But who else is bothered?

However, I have always retained the original pronunciation of my own family name, though I never make an issue of it (at the most, a mild correction when the opportunity offers). But others worry about it. Here, for example, is a very well-turned-out poem of inquiry received from Miss

Kim Whitehouse, a senior English student at a Raleigh, North Carolina, high school. It starts with "Dear Sir" and ends with "Sincerely befuddled," plus a class signature:

> We find it a shame that your name (in its fame)
> Has caused so much dispute and debating to boot
> That our tempers grew hot (ought we not be distraught?)
> So we felt that we'd better ask *you* in a letter . . .
> "It's plain to see it's 'Pea,' " said one she
> (With an all-knowing nod), "as in pod."
> "Pea my eye—it's 'Pie'!" cried I
> (Sounding clever and smart), "as in tart!"
> "No!" hollered one scholar (quite red round the collar),
> "It's 'Pay,' as one does with a dime or a dollar!"
> So please, Mr. Mario "Pea," "Pie," or "Pay,"
> Rid our wits of these nits! Tell us, what do *you* say?

The only thing to do was to reply in kind. So off went this message in verse to the young lady in Raleigh:

> Who should be to blame if a family name
> Causes friction and ructions and rifts?
> There's EYE-ther and EE-ther, but Pei rhymes with neither,
> Being one of inherited gifts.
> In the tongue of Cathay, "pei" sounds as in "pay,"
> As it does in most lingos Romance;
> It's a Catalan name that to Italy came
> Around seventeen hundred, by chance.
> Both those languages say that the sound is like "pay,"
> And to ancestry faith must be kept;
> So I keep saying "pay" right down to this day,
> Since in languages I'm an adept.

There was a further explanation in prose to the effect that Pei is used as a family name both in Chinese (the meaning of the character used is "long robe" or "scholar") and in the Catalan of northeastern Spain, which is where the family is said to have originated, moving first to South America, then to Rome at the beginning of the eighteenth century. The Catalan name is supposed to have been derived from Latin *pedinum*, infantryman, foot soldier, which in Catalan development wears down to Pey or Pei. In the Barcelona phone directory I once came across nearly a full page of Pey's and Pei's, but none are left in Italy today. I came to the United States in 1908 at the age of seven. I never cared to change my name, but take it in stride when people mispronounce it ("pie" is the most frequent mispronunciation, with *ei* pronounced German style). Since not too many know about the Catalan name, while there are several Chinese Pei's in the New York directory, I am most often taken for a Chinese, until I am seen. There is at Columbia University a distinguished Chinese professor of architecture, I. M. Pei, with whom I am often confused.

This particular inquiry made me both proud and happy; the latter, because it indicated that the spirit of research and inquiry is far from dead among our younger generations, so often unjustly berated in haphazard and hasty generalizations.

The gentle art of punning (definitely a weasely practice; "pun," said to be derived from Italian *puntiglio,* "fine point,") is traceable as an institution all the way back to Homer, Aristophanes, and Cicero (*paronophilia* is the Greek name for it, while the Romans used their own *facetiae* or the Greek-borrowed *logos*). The pun in modern politics is discussed at length by Stefan Kanfer in a *Time* Essay (February 28, 1972). Here the advantage in alliteration which the Republicans, in the person of Vice-President Agnew, have over the Democrats is nullified by Muskie's superiority over Nixon. As against the former Democratic candidate's "We just Concord the statehouse" (uttered in Concord, New Hampshire), "Mosque-Cow" (for Nasser's burial place), "Well, Soviet" ("so be it") for the Russian refusal to issue visas to his press entourage, and countless others, all we have for Nixon is "the kindest thing I had happen, even though it's crewel," upon receiving a stitched seal from daughter Julie.

McGovern, in Alaska, tried to silence a fellow candidate's supporters with "Hush, you Muskies!" Other quotable gems are Adlai Stevenson's definition of Goldwater as "one who thinks everything will be better in the rear future"; Roosevelt's "Drain Trust" for his own chosen advisers, and "Age of Chiselry" (though some attribute this to Walter Winchell); "England's Jew d'Esprit" for Disraeli; Dorothy Parker's "Chasing Rimbauds" in describing her own poetry. There is Alexander Woolcott's description of a fancy cat hospital as "charging four dollars a weak purr," and Heywood Broun's Prohibition-days coinage "Any Port in a storm."

Verily, to quote Vladimir Nabokov, "the pun is mightier than the word."

20

In Retrospect

When *Words in Sheep's Clothing* appeared in 1969, several questions were left unanswered. One in particular, for which I had previously sought enlightenment from my readers in a *Modern Age* article, was in connection with what my ear ("the enemy of the eye," to put the Berlitz slogan into reverse) told me was "mock one," "mock two," etc., used in aviation to denote the speed of sound. I had heard the expression repeatedly on radio and TV. I had never seen it in print. The dictionaries said nothing about it under "mock." What were its origin and precise meaning?

What I got was a flood of letters of correction and explanation from all kinds of sources—newspaper editors and book reviewers, like Paul Flowers, of the *Memphis* (Tennesee) *Commercial Appeal*, Thorpe Menn, of the *Kansas City* (Missouri) *Star*, James Clemon, of the *Omaha* (Nebraska) *World-Herald;* book publishers, like my own editor, Tom Sloane, of Doubleday, and Ralph De Sola, of

Better Books, San Diego; university professors, like Robert L. Benjamin, of San Diego State College, and Paul S. Boyer, of Franklin and Marshall College, Lancaster, Pennsylvania; knowledgeable laymen, like Justin Blackwelder, of Washington, D.C., John W. Robbins, of Baltimore, Maryland, Gary V. Stone, of Albuquerque, New Mexico, Charles E. Petten, of New York City, G. R. Flynn, of Seattle, Washington, A. I. Goldberg, of Rhinebeck, New York, George W. Price, of Chicago, Jack Belck, of Morgantown, West Virginia. Without exception, they set me right. It was not "mock," but "Mach," and it appeared in every dictionary (if I looked for it in the wrong spot, that was my fault, not the dictionary's). The name was that of an Austrian physicist and engineer who had first established the ratio of the speed of a plane to the speed of sound. "Mach One" meant at the speed of sound; "Mach Two," at twice the speed of sound; and so on. A couple of my correspondents brought out the fact that this was not an absolute speed, but one that might vary with local weather conditions. One stated that while the name was commonly pronounced "mock" in America, the pronunciation "mack" was more current in Britain.

I thanked my correspondents, but countered with another query. Why is the name not pronounced with its proper German pronunciation, all the more since there is a precedent in the name of the composer Johann Sebastian Bach, which musical announcers regularly utter with the broad *a* of "father" and the velar spirant *kh*-sound at the end? The man from Morgantown replied: "Since the illiterati (who are in the majority) call Bach 'Bock,' on those rare occasions when one has heard of the man, we come right back to the 'Mock' you cited." I was still unconvinced and decided to try it out on my graduate English class at Seton Hall, composed of people who were all literate. Not only would they not say "Batch," I thought; they wouldn't even say "Bock." I polled them, confidently expecting them to say "Bach." To my dismay, the majority said "Bock." I was licked.

Since then, I have noted the same type of mispronunciation among the newscasters, in connection with the Sikhs of India. Sikh is pronounced "sick." Shall I pun and say that this makes me Sikh? Is the sound that the dictionaries describe as the *ch* of Scottish "loch" so difficult to pronounce that it must be distorted? There the matter rests. But at least I am enlightened.

But the matter did not rest there with some of my correspondents, who had queries or gripes of their own. Mr. De Sola, for instance, remarked that despite the fact that he is the compiler of an *Abbreviations Dictionary,* he deplores the proliferation of phony and weasel words: "We are surrounded by sophomoric people who believe that creating abbreviations and acronyms certifies whatever intellectual and academic attainment they think they possess," he concludes.

Mr. Blackwelder denounced the gobbledegook of Washington, citing some horrible examples: "optimalization," "dialoguing," "orientated," "overview," "remediation," "practicum," "self-actualization," "latent potential."

Mr. Price was annoyed by "spacewalk" and "spacewalking"; he would prefer the old science fiction "floating," and the old "spaceman" to "astronaut."

Mr. Belck, criticizing the lingo of today's econo-sociometricians, objected to "disemployment," "dysfunction," "out migrate" and "in migrate," "deviation tolerance" (for permissiveness), "anesthesiologist" for "anesthetist" (he claims this is because medics can't pronounce the latter word; but if this is true, how can they pronounce the former?). "Garbage and fillers" are the terms he uses in connection with "larger social context," "life situational factors," "behavioral and value styles," "structural dependency," "in the school situation," "value systems," "understanding the key dimensions of," "feel functionally cut off," "in an industrial setting," "assumed leadership roles," "in a broader sense," "in depth," "in this context," and "enriched" (except when used with bread). The do-gooders, he concludes, can write Galbraithian gilt or Mailerian mud, but the conservative camp allows but two approaches, arch, *à la National Review,* or arcane, *à la Modern Age;* and he deplores the fact that there are no vulgate conservative bibles, while Lenny Bruce is more than a match for Jefferson on TV.

Mr. Menn, of the *Kansas City Star,* gently took me to task for not looking up "mini" and "family" (in the Cosa Nostra sense) in American Heritage, forgetting that the 1969 American Heritage was not available to me when I was compiling in 1968 my own 1969 article and volume. Professor Benjamin pointed out that "merger" and "conglomerate" are not synonymous, the former referring to a process, the latter to a product, with the further note that only some mergers result in conglomerates (I am still a bit confused). Mr. Flowers, of the *Memphis Commercial Appeal,* remarked that "wool hat boys" was popular during Ole Gene Talmadge's political career in Georgia, helping him defeat Atlanta's favorites under the old county unit rule. He then proceeded to introduce his own creation, "geriatric psychedelesis," which he defined as a change in personality induced by advancing years. Lastly, Mr. Goldberg suggested that "shticks" may be derived from *schtickl,* apposite to Vienna German *bissl,* bit or piece, a diminutive of *Stück,* with appropriate Yiddishization (but see pages 24 f).

There were other terms for which I had cried for help. One was "Old Glory" for our Flag. Here two correspondents, Eunice Turner, of Warren, Maine, and Jane Battersby, of Port Credit, Ontario, came to my rescue. Both tell substantially the same story. Miss Turner gives as her source a book entitled *The Flag of the United States,* by Colonel James A. Moss, published by the U.S. Flag Association of Washington; while Mrs. Battersby gives *The Story of the American Flag,* by Wayne Hipple, published in 1910 by the Henry Altemus Company, of Philadelphia. In 1824 (according to Miss Turner's authority) or in 1831 (according to Mrs. Battersby's), Captain William Driver, a shipmaster of Salem, Massachusetts, was presented with a large, beautiful American flag (the Hipple account says by a party of friends, the Moss account by his mother and a group of girls) as he was about to sail for the South Seas. When the flag was unfurled on the mast and waving in the breeze, Captain Driver exclaimed "I name her Old Glory!" Miss Turner further states that this particular flag is now in the Smithsonian Institution in Washington, preserved under glass. Not such a "closely guarded secret" after all, she banters, consoling me, however, with the added thought that James Whitcomb Riley, in his poem "The Name of Old Glory," shows in the line "Who gave you, Old Glory, the name that you bear?" as much ignorance as I did.

A truly closely guarded secret remains: the origin of "fuzz" for police. A former student of mine, David Shulman, of Donail Publications, reminds me that as far back as 1929 Eric Partridge gave the earliest quote (thereby eliminating the hippies as its source), with the remark "It is likely that 'fuzz' was originally 'fuss'—one hard to please or over-particular." Partridge, however, does not mention this use of "fuzz" in his 1958 *Origins.* Shulman adds two other educated guesses: that "fuzz" may be a corruption of "force" (police force), or that the police would resemble fuzz that clings to a person because of their persistence. It's still anyone's guess.

Mr. Petten, one of my correspondents on "Mach," also offers a suggestion on "pussycat," which he says has overtones of "pussy," slang for female private parts, and "at odds with cat and chick." At the same time, he reminds me of what he calls the "*Esquire* syndrome" for four-letter words, disguised in print into "ffing" or "effing." Mrs. Margaret Bisbee, of Carlisle, Massachusetts, commenting on the application of "pussycat" to a male, says: "A pussycat is a very, undoubtedly virile, attractive man who might be compared to a prowling, roaring tiger, but who is known or thought to be a real softie of a delightful kind by the feminine describer; there is also a hint that the person using the term has near-exclusive knowledge of this, a touch of pride, a bit of condescension; it's one of the more fascinating words to watch in use."

Both Mrs. Bisbee and Maurice Dunbar, of Mission, Texas, correct my impression that "hung" referring to male genital parts is as recent as I made it seem, with my reference to its appearance in the writings of Gore Vidal. The former tells me that the word was used by Thomas Wolfe in his "three o'clock" reminiscences in *The Web and the Rock*. The latter remembers the term being used among farm boys when he was a child; it was used, he adds, in the Southwest at least fifty years ago with reference to a bull or a stallion, and a common simile applied to a man is "hung like a stud horse." The same writer offers a correction in connection with "wildcat oil well," which he says is now used for a producing well drilled in unproved territory, and more or less synonymous with "speculative." "Gusher," he adds, best conveys the meaning I attributed to "wildcat" (a well that spouts when it isn't wanted to).

Gerard Harrington, Managing Editor of the *Meriden* (Connecticut) *Morning Record,* disagrees with the rather tentative dictionary etymologies of "scram" from "scramble" or German *schrammen,* and suggests that it is a modification of "screw" used in its slangy, obscene sense, which, he claims, developed the secondary meaning of "get the hell out of here." Around 1927, when he heard "scram" used in the same double function, he asked an in-group bartender and was told: "It's only 'screw' wid a college education." Wentworth and Flexner give both "scram" and "screw" in the sense of "get out" from the early 1930s. They do not set a date for "screw" in the obscene sense, but imply that it is quite old. They do not mention an obscene sense for "scram." Neither does American Heritage, the most recent of our dictionaries.

Mrs. Margaret Nickerson, of Greenville, Delaware, resents the implication that the Colonial Dames are descended from supporters of King George III. Rather, she says, they are descended from ancestors who were here some time before the Revolution and held posts of importance in the colonies. Her own eligibility to the Dames is due to the arrival of an ancestor in 1635 and his fathering a line of hardworking, capable men, one of whom was a Warden of Connecticut (whatever that meant, she adds). The Dames are fiercely patriotic, she assures me; but of that there was never any question.

I am taken to task by Miss Betty Adler, librarian of the Enoch Pratt Free Library, Baltimore, Maryland, which specializes in Menckeniana, for failing to report my good friend H. L. Mencken as the coiner of "ecdysiast." I blush to admit that she is perfectly right. The story of Mencken's coining of the word appears on page 584 ff. of Supplement I of his *American Language,* a book that I treasure and once reviewed. My abject apologies for the oversight.

For the derivation of "hooligan" from the family name Hoolihan, E. H. Conroy, of St. John's, Newfoundland, suggests Spanish *holgazán* (lazy) instead, though he admits that the spelling Houlighan is occasionally found for Houlihan. At the same time, he deplores the confusion between "careen" and "career," and the use of "decimate" in the sense of almost annihilate, along with "presently" for "now," and of the coinage "ideate." "Now" as an adjective reminds Attorney Charles Van Patten, of New York City, that "once" as an adjective appears in the title of T. S. White's novel *The Once and Future King*. Bettyanne Galloway, of Bucknell College, deplores two euphemisms in use there: "Director of Alumni Relations" for Alumni Secretary, and "Campus Security" for Campus Police. Harry Burdick, of Montclair, New Jersey, similarly deplores the use of "inner city," a term appearing in antiquity and the Middle Ages to describe the citadel of the castle, the place for last-ditch defense, as a euphemism for a slum area. (The term, incidentally, appears in none of our dictionaries.)

The term "catawampus," which was the subject of an inquiry conducted by Winifred Warren, of North Pomfret, Vermont, did not appear in our earlier volume, but seems to be a native American coinage of the same time as "rambunctious" and "cantankerous." The few dictionaries that carry it (Webster Third and American Heritage) describe it as a cross between "catamount" and "catacorner," and give its various meanings as fierce, destructive, malicious, an imaginary animal or hobgoblin, askew, awry, confused, mixed up. It looked interesting enough to be picked up by Dickens in 1842 and by Bulwer-Lytton in 1853. A fitting monument to American linguistic creativity and linguistic interest.

Index of Persons, Places, Titles, and Things

The author wishes to acknowledge his indebtedness to his many sources, chief among them the standard dictionaries used in this study: *The Shorter Oxford English Dictionary* (Clarendon, Oxford, England, 1955 ed.); *Webster's Third New International Dictionary* (G. & C. Merriam Company, Springfield, Massachusetts, 1961 ed.); *The Random House Dictionary of the English Language* (Random House, New York, 1966); *The American Heritage Dictionary of the English Language* (American Heritage Publishing Company, New York, 1969); and one specialized work, H. Wentworth and S. B. Flexner, *Dictionary of American Slang* (Thomas Y. Crowell Company, New York, 1960). These are so often referred to in the text that it would have been impractical to list page references for them in the following index. Other works less frequently mentioned and their authors are indexed both under their titles and under their authors: for example, "Safire, William" and *New Language of Politics, The* refer to William Safire, *The New Language of Politics*, revised and enlarged edition (New York, Collier, 1972). Newspaper- and magazine-writers are listed, with separate entries for the periodicals where their material appeared. There is also occasional reference to items of general interest, such as prefixes, suffixes, foreign languages, etc.; and to the originators, real or supposed, of individual words and expressions. Titles of relevant radio and television programs and of songs are listed as well. I also wish to acknowledge my indebtedness to *Modern Age* magazine for permission to include, with minor changes, the article "The Language of Taxation" (Spring 1972) as Chapter 10 of this book; to the members of one of my graduate English classes at Seton Hall University, who were of great assistance in the compilation of Chapters 17 and 18; and to the numerous friends and correspondents who supplied me with abundant material for Chapter 20.

Index of Words and Expressions